"Mark Teasdale's new book comes at the rig[...] everywhere are challenged to find timely expressions of the gospel. Without a clear and holistic understanding of what *salvation* means in our day and age, churches will struggle in ministry and mission in their given contexts. *Participating in Abundant Life* follows a positive approach and is deeply encouraging reading—rooted in Scripture, theologically comprehensive, and convincingly clear in its conclusions. It is a highly recommend resource for students of theology and evangelism as well as for clergy and lay leaders with a 'bias for the gospel.'"

Achim Härtner, academic dean and E. Stanley Jones Professor of Evangelism at Reutlingen School of Theology, Germany

"Mark skillfully widens the scope of salvation—connecting back to the concepts of *shalom* and the kingdom of God—to show that a more holistic and yet deeply biblical view of abundant and eternal life is for both the world now and the world to come. So good, and a much-needed word for the times we're living in."

James Choung, author of *True Story: A Christianity Worth Believing In*

"Dr. Teasdale powerfully connects the heart cry of contemporary culture for justice and flourishing with a biblical and much-needed expanded soteriology. *Participating in the Abundant Life* lifts up the important work of 'common good' missiology for both restoring the relevance of evangelism in the church as well as the relevance of the Christian message for those outside it. Dr. Teasdale's vision of evangelism gives the right attention to the human relevance of a gospel that transcends the captivity it has fallen into through the various echo chambers of faith traditions in the West, rightly reminding us that Jesus saves both from the hell to come as well as the hell that is now."

R. York Moore, executive director for catalytic partnerships and national evangelist, InterVarsity Christian Fellowship/USA

"When I read Mark Teasdale's *Participating in Abundant Life*, I found myself immersed in a text devoted to a holistic understanding of salvation amid a global context. A text developed during a global pandemic and cultural upheaval, this book articulates a coherent expression of salvation that goes beyond eternal rewards and reminds us of redemption in our everyday contexts. Through Teasdale's approach, the reader can engage with a range of thinkers and theologians in exploring a fully developed view of salvation. As a pastor who frequently looks for texts to provide parishioners with breadth and depth of engagement, I find Teasdale's book to be exactly the kind I enjoy putting into their hands. This versatile text is useful both in the classrooms of higher education institutions and around small group circles in local churches. Being able to read about the greater hope of our salvation, done within an ecumenical conversation, gives us a greater encouragement to share the news of Jesus Christ. I am sure this book will benefit many more and help grow God's kingdom."

Garet D. Robinson, pastor of adult ministries at University Baptist Church, Houston

Participating in Abundant Life

*Holistic Salvation
for a Secular Age*

Mark R. Teasdale

ivp
Academic
An imprint of InterVarsity Press
Downers Grove, Illinois

InterVarsity Press
P.O. Box 1400, Downers Grove, IL 60515-1426
ivpress.com
email@ivpress.com

InterVarsity Press® is the book-publishing division of InterVarsity Christian Fellowship/USA®, a movement of students and faculty active on campus at hundreds of universities, colleges, and schools of nursing in the United States of America, and a member movement of the International Fellowship of Evangelical Students. For information about local and regional activities, visit intervarsity.org.

While any stories in this book are true, some names and identifying information may have been changed to protect the privacy of individuals.

The publisher cannot verify the accuracy or functionality of website URLs used in this book beyond the date of publication.

Cover design and image composite: David Fassett
Interior design: Daniel van Loon
Images: plant wall: © 4045 / iStock / Getty Images Plus
*   leaves with tendril: © firina / iStock / Getty Images Plus*

ISBN 978-1-5140-0052-6 (print)
ISBN 978-1-5140-0053-3 (digital)

Printed in the United States of America ♾

InterVarsity Press is committed to ecological stewardship and to the conservation of natural resources in all our operations. This book was printed using sustainably sourced paper.

Library of Congress Cataloging-in-Publication Data

A catalog record for this book is available from the Library of Congress.

P 25 24 23 22 21 20 19 18 17 16 15 14 13 12 11 10 9 8 7 6 5 4 3 2 1

Y 42 41 40 39 38 37 36 35 34 33 32 31 30 29 28 27 26 25 24 23 22

To Ana, who has long shown me what it means to be passionate

about the mission of improving the lives of others.

To missionaries everywhere and across history

who have learned to offer a full witness to the gospel

no matter the context in which they serve.

Contents

Foreword by Alan Hirsch and
Mark Nelson | *ix*

Acknowledgments | *xiii*

Introduction | *1*

1 A Mission for the Common Good | *7*

2 Experiencing Salvation | *28*

3 Saving Lives | *59*

4 Standard of Living | *79*

5 Saving Happiness | *106*

6 Eternal Life | *135*

7 Salvation Today | *161*

Appendix: Metrics for Salvation | *173*

General Index | *205*

Scripture Index | *209*

Foreword

Alan Hirsch and Mark Nelson

IMAGINE YOURSELF, some two thousand years ago, standing at the edge of the water, straining to hear the words of a random teacher from rural Nazareth (who for some reason was standing in a boat) as he speaks to a surprisingly large crowd. You are not able to hear much of what he says, just bits and pieces. Or envision coming upon a man that you *know* had been paralyzed for thirty plus years and is now, with his mat under his arm, walking down the street talking about this same Nazarene who had asked him, "Do you want to be whole?" and then evidently healed him. Or further still, picture yourself coming upon a crowd whispering and murmuring about a confrontation just minutes before: angry religious leaders, tossing about a woman caught with a man who was not her husband, publicly confronting that same Nazarene teacher with hopes of trapping him with his own words. (They not only didn't trap him, but they had also disappeared into the crowd either indignant or embarrassed.)

Again and again, you have stumbled upon this man named Jesus with hopes of gaining a fuller understanding of what he's *really* about, wanting to grasp the entirety of this message that so many are being drawn to. And with the small portions you have gleaned, you find yourself desperate for more of this news that he seems to be offering. You find yourself longing for the whole picture. The entire story. What is it exactly that Jesus came to embody and enact in this world, and why does he seem to offer something that no one else does?

Jesus came to tell and embody the story of God. He came to give the whole picture—"I am going to put it all together, pull it all together in a vast panorama" (Matthew 5:17, *The Message*). There is to be no partial viewing; no one should have a seat with a restricted view. Anything less than a full viewing experience is a cause for lament.

It is this *whole picture* of Jesus and the life he offers and calls us to that is the subject of this book. Mark Teasdale has taken on the grand task of bringing us into an understanding of the whole picture that Jesus came to show us. A picture that calls us toward a life that you will soon be convinced is best described as "abundant."

The quest for abundant life that every person pursues (regardless of their belief system or whether they acknowledge the search) proves elusive again and again. Simply survey the current age we find ourselves living in. We have lost our sense of the bigger picture that Jesus laid out before us and find ourselves perfecting the art of settling for something *far less* than abundant. As the writer Walker Percy describes, "Ours is the only civilization in history which has enshrined mediocrity as its cultural ideal."[1] This book calls us out of the restricted view of mediocre life and toward abundance. Not toward a better life that is simply another chapter in self-fulfillment and self-actualization, but toward a life that is a fuller expression of the gospel and the fuller picture that Jesus came to bring. It is a picture of participating in abundant life that is not *either-or* but *both-and*—the eternal *and* the immediate; being loved *and* being loving; a deeper knowledge *and* a more expansive lived expression; holistic *and* missional; being transformed individually *and* communally; pursuing both the individual good *and* the common good; receiving grace *and* sharing grace; believing the resurrection *and* living the resurrection.

---

[1] Walker Percy, *The Moviegoer* (New York: Random House, 1961), 223.

This is the picture that Mark Teasdale paints so beautifully throughout this entire book. He artfully focuses on a broader, deeper, and wider view of salvation deeply rooted in Scripture that is not restricted by contextual divides, while at the same time calling us to account for how we embody abundant life by establishing measurables for each of us regardless of our contexts.

As you read, may you allow yourself to be led by the Spirit in a search to experience and participate in this abundant life, to pursue a view of the entire picture that Jesus came to bring that leads us beyond our settled convictions and toward a wholeness we may have never imagined existed.

Acknowledgments

THE IDEA FOR THIS BOOK, that the salvific work of God through Christ includes working for the common good, developed over numerous years and came as a result of several interactions that I have had with people. It would be impossible to acknowledge all of them, but there are three in particular worthy of note.

It is thanks to my mother that I began to understand Christian mission as something that extends beyond what we do within the local church. Indeed, it is when we work to make an impact for good in the larger culture around us that we are truly living into our calling as Christians.

It is thanks to my father that I began to realize that we continue to play a part in the unfolding story of the Bible. The Scriptures are not just an old book that offers us guidance but a living story that we are characters in today.

It is especially thanks to my wife, Ana, who read and reread this manuscript to make certain that I was being faithful to the logic and practices of humanitarian aid organizations. Ana has spent her entire professional life working for organizations that deal with providing humanitarian aid or promoting civil society and public policy. This has taken her around the world, including into dangerous and war-torn areas. Watching her travel to these places helped me realize that those who do this work, regardless of their faith, are exemplars of at least some of the Beatitudes. In particular, the aid workers she witnessed in Iraq in the days immediately following the Second Gulf War, who wended their way through

M16-wielding soldiers and routine terrorist attacks to provide needed assistance to those suffering, are worthy of being called "peacemakers."

Two colleagues at Garrett-Evangelical Theological Seminary were instrumental in helping me go deeper into the biblical literature about salvation: K. K. Yeo, the Harry R. Kendall Professor of New Testament, and G. Brooke Lester, Associate Professor of Hebrew Scriptures. Both provided me with crash courses in the core themes and authors related to their respective testaments of expertise.

Thanks to the Dakotas, Minnesota, and Arkansas Annual Conferences of The United Methodist Church, who agreed to have groups of pastors "beta test" the score cards in the appendix.

A final note of thanks to Jon Boyd of InterVarsity Press. Jon saw promise in this project years before it was ready to see the light of day as a book. It is thanks to his gentle direction and perseverance that the book found its way from being a proposal in desperate need of revision, to a manuscript, to what you have in your hands.

Introduction

I WAS SITTING ACROSS THE TABLE FROM EVENS PAUL, a former student of mine and the cofounder and director of SAI-Haiti. Evens is a remarkable young man; truth be told, the seminary needs him much more for his spiritual vitality than he needs the seminary. I certainly always felt like I learned more from him in my classes than I ever was able to teach!

A native of La Victoire, Haiti, Evens was able to attend college in Haiti and later in the United States (thanks to his parents, who had saved money for him), allowing him to earn bachelor's degrees in both agriculture and theology as well as a master's degree in Christian education. I originally met him when he was a student in my seminary class. Now, three years later, he had graduated and was going back to take over hands-on leadership of SAI-Haiti, which he had been running at a distance for nearly eight years.

By this point in our conversation, Evens had long since lost interest in the chicken sandwich on the plate in front of him. He was engrossed in sharing his vision for what he hoped to accomplish in La Victoire. Describing especially the plight of the children, he explained how the town is so remote that basic necessities, schools, and medical facilities are difficult to access. People commonly have pronounced cheekbones due to malnutrition. They receive only a few years of education. Illiteracy is rampant. Those who are sick struggle to find transportation to visit a doctor or hospital in the cities several miles away.

Having laid out these ills, Evens enthusiastically shared how he would help his fellow Haitians. He wanted to make certain that every child had enough to eat. He would do this through handouts but also, more importantly, through teaching sustainable agricultural practices so the people could grow their food over time. He would make certain every child had a decent education so they could improve their and their families' situations, a dream he had already started to see come to fruition when he reported that three hundred students had attended a school he had helped establish. He planned on purchasing a bus to help carry people from La Victoire into the cities as well as to bring mission teams back.

There was more. Evens had launched SAI-Haiti by planting a church in La Victoire. In addition to directing the humanitarian work, he was serving as the senior pastor at the church. In this role, his primary desire was to evangelize people in the town, sharing the gospel of Jesus Christ so that people had hope both now and for eternity. He did not want to do this work alone but hoped to establish training sessions on evangelism for the pastors in the region. He wanted to equip them with clearer theology and better practices of ministry so they would be more effective in making disciples of Jesus Christ.

As I listened to Evens, inspired by his enthusiasm, a thought suddenly came to me. "You're talking about salvation, aren't you?" I said, "But this salvation is not just getting people to share in the glories of heaven or helping their suffering bodies on earth. It involves both." "Yes!" he replied, "I want people to know God's blessing to be saved from hunger, ignorance, and want. I also want them to know God's salvation as the hope of glory for eternity in the presence of God."

Upon hearing this, I asked him if I could include our exchange in this book!

Evens's answer makes sense. Virtually every Christian I know would hear this and respond, "Of course! Of course God wants people to share in God's blessings both now and into eternity. Of course God wants people to have healthy, strong bodies as well as eternal life that will persist beyond our mortal death, caught up in the abundant grace of God."

Christians aren't the only people to think this. Others, whether they hold to another faith or no faith at all, would at least agree that people should have access to decent food, water, hygiene, shelter, education, medical care, and other necessities of life. People should be able to live without the fear that they or their children would be caught in an unending cycle of poverty. And, when the time comes, people should be able to face death with dignity. Those outside the Christian faith may not agree with the focus on Jesus or the church, but they could support the improvements that Evens was accomplishing for people in this world.

While we might all agree on these things, rarely would we talk about all of them in terms of salvation. For some Christians, the term *salvation* is not appropriately applied to meeting physical needs. For others, the notion of salvation has too much baggage regarding sin and judgment to be useful. For those who hold to no faith, the word *salvation* likely would not come to mind at all.

This book steps in to address this lack of soteriological imagination by helping us think of salvation as something we experience by participating in abundant life. Abundant life helps us understand how much God wants to save us from and how holistically God wants to bless us. It also is a term that people of goodwill can rally around regardless of their religiosity or secularity.

My hope is that all people of goodwill, whether Christian, adherents of other religions, or secular, can look at the people of La Victoire and agree with Evens that they need salvation as expressed in the term *abundant life*. More than this, my hope is that all these people will be able to link hands with someone like Evens to participate in abundant life.[1]

---

[1] You can learn more about Sustainable Action International-Haiti at https://sai-haiti.org/.

OF PANDEMICS AND PROTESTS

As I was working on this manuscript, two things burst onto the global scene. First, Covid-19 made its entrance, leading to months of quarantine, the rise of new terminology such as "social distancing" and "flattening the curve," and a reassessment of how people should relate to each other outside of the home. Lurking behind all of this was the fear of a new, highly infectious, little understood, constantly mutating, and deadly virus.

Just as many of the quarantines were beginning to lift in the United States, George Floyd was killed by a police officer in Minneapolis. This ignited a wave of protests that swept across the nation and the world. Pent-up outrage over the inequities and violence that Black Americans face because of the structural racism in the United States led to demands for justice on local and national levels.

In both cases, it is not too much to say that what people desired, regardless of faith commitment, was abundant life. Everyone touched by the Covid-19 pandemic would have lived more fully if someone—anyone—could have cured the virus and immunized the global population from it. Those who lost their employment or had their salaries cut would have fuller lives if there was a sudden return of their jobs and income. People struggling with the intense loneliness and depression caused by being in isolation would have experienced fuller life in being free to gather with their friends and family again. Students forced to study at home, especially those who did not have access to personal electronics or the internet, would have known a fuller life if they could have received their education in school. People of color who disproportionately suffered from the virus would have found a fuller life if they had equal access to medical facilities and employment that did not require them to be in harm's way. In each case, they would have been saved from a death-dealing situation to enjoy greater blessings in life.

The protests for racial justice were likewise a call for abundant life to be equally available for all people. It would save the United States from a legal system that allows for racism at the point of encounter between Black Americans and police as well as at the point of sentencing those who have been convicted. It would save Black children from the cradle-to-prison infrastructure that begins with the educational achievement gap. It would invest in all neighborhoods, giving equal opportunity to people of all colors to build wealth and pass that wealth to the next generation unhindered by redlining, predatory lending practices, or discriminatory hiring and promotions. All of this would rescue the nation from practices that diminish or destroy life and would allow people to live more abundantly.

Both the pandemic and the protests reinforced the need for a more holistic understanding of salvation that entails every aspect of human experience. People are crying out not just for hope at the end of our mortal lives but for life itself.

People of color have long pointed to the need for our view of salvation to include life in this world and the next. James Cone, the father of Black theology and an alumni of Garrett-Evangelical, where I teach, made this point in an article titled "Evangelization and Politics: A Black Perspective." In it he argued the church's evangelistic efforts are defined by its understanding of salvation. He then demonstrated that the biblical witness consistently presents salvation as a political act of liberation "in history" as well as a promise of the eschatological "home over yonder."[2] Drawing these ideas together offers a picture of abundant life.

What sounded revolutionary to quarters of the church when Cone penned this in the 1970s has become more acceptable in the 2020s. It is also accessible to those who are outside the Christian faith. The time to present the idea of experiencing salvation as participating in the abundant life of Christ has come. I hope this book provides the basis for the church, especially the White church in the United States, to have

---

[2]James H. Cone, "Evangelization and Politics: A Black Perspective," in *Black Theology: A Documentary History, 1966–1979,* ed. Gayraud S. Wilmore and James H. Cone (Maryknoll, NY: Orbis Books, 1993), 531-42.

its soteriology expanded by this idea. In doing this, I also hope that the local church's practice of ministry, including evangelism, will offer a far better witness to how Jesus Christ invites us not just to *receive* but to *enact* abundant life.

1

A Mission for the Common Good

SINCE I BEGAN TEACHING EVANGELISM over a decade ago, I have pushed my students to explain their "starting point."[1] Their starting point is the good thing God has done in their lives through Jesus Christ that they want others to experience. This is an alternative to popular conceptions of evangelism, which are grounded in preparing for judgment (rather than being invited into God's goodness) and are rehearsed as a pat set of propositional statements Christians have memorized about God's love (rather than being shared out of the Christian's personal experience of God's grace).

Once my students can articulate their respective starting points, they need to expand on them. Instead of just seeing their experiences as one-off moments or feelings, they need to use them as the basis for explaining the nature of God and how God interacts with the world. Who is the God that brings about the kind of goodness they experienced? What activities does this God engage in? How does this God want us to respond to this goodness? The starting point becomes the foundation for making sense of their individual life stories and, more broadly, for developing a metanarrative that makes sense of how God operates in the universe.[2]

---

[1]This is the first component of my "evangelism equation": starting point + theological reflection + contextual awareness = creative practices. My book *Evangelism for Non-Evangelists* (Downers Grove, IL: InterVarsity Press, 2016) walks through the equation in detail.

[2]Essential to this process is theological reflection, which requires people to develop their metanarrative in a way that is accountable to the teachings of Scripture and the tradition of the church. This is not just a process of creating personalized versions of the gospel and passing them off as the Christian faith!

This metanarrative stretches across time. It tells the story of how God has worked to bring goodness in the past, how God is sustaining goodness in the present, and how the student anticipates with hope the goodness God will bring in the future, even into eternity. This story provides the motivation for the students' life choices and ministries. It also is something they want others to know and claim so they can enjoy the goodness God offers.

It is at the point of shifting from their personal experiences to a metanarrative that my students often stumble. They understand the need to articulate their authentic experience of God's goodness through Jesus, but they have trouble seeing how this launches them to a grander view of the goodness that God wants all people to experience. They struggle to articulate how God's actions in the past and present lead to a vision for God's purposes in the future.

My students are not alone. Many Christians have trouble explaining this. As an evangelism professor, I often run across this. A recent email from a pastor asking me to develop a training program stated this explicitly. When I asked him whether he wanted me to focus more on evangelistic theology or evangelistic practices, he replied,

> I'm asking for even one step further back. As the pastor here, I am very concerned that even our leaders and staff can't articulate faith succinctly or confidently. We have some of the best people in the world here at [First Church], but we aren't at all confident at faith sharing. We can run meetings, we can set agendas, we can be good citizens, we are great at serving in various ways, but if someone asks even our leaders and staff to share about their faith, there is fear and trepidation showing in our eyes.

This pastor's plea catches the Zeitgeist of many congregations in the West today. We know how to do good things. We know we should do them in Jesus' name. We know we have hope for eternity. We don't know how to fit all these pieces together; much less do we have a coherent explanation for why they ought to fit together. As Alan Hirsch and Mark Nelson astutely observed in their book *Reframation*: "We have lost a sense of the big story that makes sense of all our little stories."[3]

REINTRODUCING SALVATION

The Christian concept that expresses how God works to overcome all harm and bring goodness to creation is salvation. This makes the concept of salvation indispensable to sharing our faith since it explains both the dangers God desires to save us from and the goodness God desires to grant us. It plants a flag in the ground that declares unequivocally that Christians believe God is good and that God works to share that goodness with all people. As clear as this seems to be, I am convinced that it is a lack of clarity about what we believe salvation is that has brought Christians to this discomfort in sharing their faith.

Even though the word *salvation* is ubiquitous in Christian teaching, it is often left undefined. The result is for Christians to have this centerpiece of their faith shrink in importance and scope. It becomes reduced to an agenda that is more defined by cultural or countercultural logic than by the gospel, often made synonymous with concepts such as justice, equality, or soul-saving. Outside of this, it is a vague hope that may provide solace at a funeral but has little impact on daily life.

Compounding this lack of clarity is that Christians in the West live in a secular culture. Per Charles Taylor's work, this is a culture that sets up an "immanent frame"[4] which disallows any consideration of the supernatural, much less of the full Christian gospel. Being motivated

---

[3]Alan Hirsch and Mark Nelson, *Reframation: Seeing God, People, and Mission Through Reenchanted Frames* (Los Angeles: 100 Movements Publishing, 2019), 48.

[4]Charles Taylor, *A Secular Age* (Cambridge, MA: Belknap Press of Harvard University Press, 2007), 542. Taylor goes on to argue that this "immanent frame" pushes us toward a "closed world view" that rejects epistemological claims outside of nature (555). Having made this point, he insists that it is not inevitable. He declares, "While the norms and practices of the immanent frame may incline toward closure, this neither decides the effect that living within the frame will have on us, nor even less does it justify the closed take" (556). I pick up on this argument by suggesting a more fully biblical view that allows us to be more effective witnesses for Christ in a secular context.

by profit, power, or other earthly desires may be crass, but at least it makes sense since these are goals that the secular culture recognizes. Being motivated by the desire for people to enter the goodness of an invisible deity is not. So, we either make our belief in God vague and private to avoid having it interfere with our daily interactions with others, or we adopt a logic for salvation that fits within preexisting agendas for improving the world, convincing ourselves the parts of the gospel that are outside those agendas are anachronistic, unnecessary, or simply wrong.

There is another way, a way that provides a more holistic vision of the goodness God desires to provide through salvation and that moves Christians away from their reduced understandings of it. It is an understanding that presents salvation as something to be experienced in an ongoing way. We are not saved just once, but we enter a continuous process of receiving and sharing God's goodness, even working alongside other people of goodwill as witnesses for Christ. This is participating in abundant life.

SALVATION AS PARTICIPATING IN ABUNDANT LIFE

The term *abundant life* comes from John 10:10, when Jesus is speaking to the Pharisees about the way that the Good Shepherd approaches his sheep. The Good Shepherd enters the sheep pen through the door, demonstrating that he is the natural and rightful caretaker of the sheep. This contrasts to those who break into the pen. These people are thieves who only harm the sheep. Applying the metaphor of the Good Shepherd to himself and the metaphor of the thief to false teachers, Jesus states, "The thief comes only to steal and kill and destroy. I came that they may have life, and have it abundantly" (NRSV).

According to Jesus, the Good Shepherd comes to bring abundant life to the sheep. Following this metaphor, participating in abundant life involves two things for the sheep: being cared for by the Good Shepherd and joining the Good Shepherd in caring for others.

The Good Shepherd cares for the needs of the sheep. This includes attending to the physical and social needs of the sheep. The shepherd provides them a safe place to stay, sufficient pasture and water, and even the company of each other. The shepherd himself keeps the sheep company as seen later in the passage, when Jesus says that the sheep know his voice, suggesting that the shepherd is present with the sheep and talks with them (John 10:27).

This is not all. After introducing the term *abundant life*, Jesus refers to his coming death (John 10:11-15). He explains that, as the Good Shepherd, he must protect his sheep from the wolf that desires to destroy them. He will do this by allowing the wolf to kill him in place of the sheep. In saying this, Jesus avers that the abundant life he offers is not restricted to caring for physical needs but involves providing something that only his death could make possible. According to traditional Christian teaching, it is through his death that God provides forgiveness for sin and entrance into eternal glory. Jesus makes this eternal aspect of abundant life plain in the same passage when he states, "I give them eternal life, and they will never perish. No one will snatch them out of my hand" (John 10:28 NRSV).

Jesus is pleased to provide this abundant life to all people, just as the Good Shepherd provides it to all the sheep. Jesus is so desirous to share this abundant life with everyone that, if we borrow a passage from the Gospel of Luke, he even seeks the lost to share it with them (Luke 15:3-7). However, Jesus does not just call people to receive life. They are to join him in sharing this life with others.

A shepherd does not care for sheep just because he enjoys doing it. The shepherd cares for sheep with the expectation that the sheep will share their gifts. They will be sheared, providing wool for clothing, blankets, and other necessities. They will give milk that can nourish others. Some may even give their lives to provide meat for hungry people to eat. Notably, the sheep do nothing to earn these gifts. They simply receive them as the shepherd makes life possible for them. They then give the gifts at the time the shepherd decides.

Likewise, Jesus expects that people will share the gifts they have received from God with others, especially those who are in need. The difference is that people have far more gifts they can share than sheep have. They might provide financial assistance for the poor, food for the hungry, community for the lonely, encouragement for the brokenhearted, and the gospel message for sinners ready to repent and find eternal life. In doing this, people become more than just recipients of abundant life whom Jesus saves from harm in this world and the next; they become participants in abundant life. They allow the life they receive from Jesus to shine through them as they reach out with their gifts so that others might live more fully.

Participating in abundant life allows us to live into the entire narrative of God's salvific work in our lives. We celebrate that God did save us through Christ in the past. We look forward expectantly to the glory God will welcome us into in the future. We participate in receiving God's provision and sharing it with others in the present. We also recognize that the salvation God provides us includes caring for people in both this world and the next through the life and death of Jesus Christ. All of this has direct implications for our evangelistic witness because it calls on those of us who enjoy God's life-giving provisions to make this fullness of life available to others. The abundant life we experience through Jesus is both holistic and missional.

ABUNDANT LIFE AND THE COMMON GOOD

The idea of participating in abundant life does more than offer an expanded understanding of salvation. It also provides Christians an attractive way to express their faith within a secular context. In *For the Life of the World*, Miroslav Volf and Matthew Croasmun give two reasons for this. First, our notion of human flourishing identifies what kind of life we believe is worth living.[5] In this case, we are claiming our lives flourish best

---

[5]Miroslav Volf and Matthew Croasmun, *For the Life of the World* (Grand Rapids, MI: Brazos Press, 2019), 22.

when we participate in abundant life by receiving and sharing God's goodness with others. Second, every culture recognizes the need to have a vision of the good to order people's lives.[6] Whether our culture is secular or not, all people are seeking for a meaningful way to live. Apart from our ability to articulate our understanding of the abundant life God offers us now and into the future, along with its call to care for others, we fail to have a message that meets this existential need.

But we do have such a message, and it is compelling. While Jesus is clear that only those who follow him will inherit eternal life, he is equally clear that God sustains the lives of all people regardless of their belief or even morality. In the Sermon on the Mount he explains that God "makes his sun rise on the evil and on the good, and sends rain on the righteous and on the unrighteous" (Matthew 5:45 NRSV). This is not the fullness of abundant life, but it still is an act of common grace and is exceptionally generous. God provides vast resources to sustain the physical lives of everyone on earth.

Despite this generosity, through sin, injustice, and tragedy, many people find themselves in need. Jesus makes it clear that those who follow him are to care for these people. As we explore later, he even shares that the eternal salvation of those who have much is dependent on whether they share with those who have little.

Part of what makes this message compelling is that the idea of caring for the needs of others entails working for the common good. This is not uniquely Christian. Those who argue that all religions seem like they are the same often point to the common ethic of caring for others that most religions, as well as people who are secular, teach. We can all agree that we should feed the hungry, clothe the naked, heal the sick, visit the lonely, and work for justice. And, in fact, people of goodwill who have sufficient resources do commit to these activities regardless of their faith tradition or lack thereof.

---

[6]Volf and Croasmun, *For the Life of the World*, 19.

Rather than be concerned that acknowledging this broad human commitment to care for others dilutes the Christian message, Christians should welcome it. It demonstrates that the Spirit of God is alive and well, prompting all people at least partially to participate in abundant life. They are receiving some of God's abundant life through the provisions that sustain them in this world, and they are inspired to share these gifts with others.

This common commitment to care for others gives Christians a platform from which to share the gospel message more fully. Christians, no less than anyone else, seek to work for the common good. We agree with all those who commit themselves to saving people from hunger, destitution, pain, disease, and the other maladies that afflict creation, and we can work beside them toward this noble end. As we do this, we will gain credibility to share with them that we believe what we are doing is part of how we experience salvation: participating in the abundant life of God by receiving God's provisions and sharing them with others. We can go on to explain that we believe the abundant life God offers not only encompasses God's provisions for the common good but extends to saving people from sin and death, offering them the glory of eternity through Christ. Those we work alongside will know we are Christians not just by our words but by our loving actions toward them and toward the needy. Moreover, they will know that we believe they are not far from the kingdom of God because they have responded to the prompting of the Spirit to love their neighbors.

An objection can be raised here: Won't our understanding of salvation be diluted and commandeered by secular forces if we connect abundant life with working toward the common good? Or won't we become sell-outs that just want public acclamation and forget that we are supposed to be participants in God's mission to redeem creation through Christ? This would put us back in the position of reducing salvation to human agendas.

No. Participating in abundant life means that we believe and practice the entire gospel. The gospel proclaims that God provides abundant life to all creation through Jesus Christ in the power of the Holy Spirit.[7] This abundant life overflows into this world and the next. That means we should care for all that happens in this world, including working for the common good. It also means we do not lose sight of sin, repentance, and eternity. As we will see, the temporal and eternal forms of abundant life complement each other, creating a reinforcing logic that demands we attend to both in our Christian mission.

The Holy Spirit further vouchsafes our fidelity to the gospel. The Spirit is at work in more people than just Christians. This is why there are people of goodwill who are already being prompted to care for others even though they do not follow Christ. The Spirit both prompts the act of love for neighbor and prepares the heart of the person who is loving their neighbor to receive the gospel. The Christian who comes alongside these people of goodwill is not losing the distinctiveness of the gospel by claiming that these people are participating in abundant life through their service to neighbor. Rather, the Christian is working with the Spirit to complete what the Spirit has already begun by demonstrating belief and commitment to sharing both the physical and eternal aspects of abundant life through Christ.

To better equip Christians to share their faith by word and deed as they participate in abundant life within a secular culture, we need language to interpret our beliefs to others who are either unfamiliar with or have distorted ideas about the Christian faith. To address this, it is wise to use language that is already accepted and understood in the secular world. I suggest using the terms *standard of living, quality of life,* and *eternal life* to explain the various ways God provides abundant life.

---

[7]For my defense of this articulation of the gospel, see Mark R. Teasdale, "A Bias for the Gospel," *International Bulletin of Mission Research*, forthcoming.

STANDARD OF LIVING, QUALITY OF LIFE, AND ETERNAL LIFE

All three of these aspects of abundant life will be covered in detail in later chapters. However, a brief introduction to them along with how they connect to Christian ministry is helpful here.

Standard of living. Standard of living refers to the ability to consume what we need and want. It is usually measured both by a person's access to things they can consume and their ability to afford those things. Put simply, those with a high standard of living are rich in income and have easy access to goods and services they can purchase with that income. Those with a low standard of living are poor in income and/or do not have access to goods and services.

Jesus explicitly taught in the Sermon on the Mount that God recognizes our physical needs and cares for them: "Therefore do not worry, saying, 'What will we eat?' or 'What will we drink?' or 'What will we wear?' For it is the Gentiles who strive for all these things; and indeed your heavenly Father knows that you need all these things" (Matthew 6:31-32 NRSV). This makes it clear that the abundant life God offers includes providing for people to have a good standard of living. In addition, God does not want people to keep their provisions only for themselves. They are to share whatever physical gifts they have with those who are in need. John the Baptist explained this succinctly when the crowds asked him how to live: "Whoever has two coats must share with anyone who has none; and whoever has food must do likewise" (Luke 3:11 NRSV).

By giving of their physical means, Christians demonstrate they both have received the portion of abundant life that relates to standard of living and that they participate in abundant life by willingly sharing. Christians can do this individually, collectively, or even by working with organizations that are not expressly Christian, partnering with anyone else sharing their physical resources with those in need. This establishes an empirically verifiable and quantifiable platform from which Christians share the good news in word and deed.

The United Nations' Human Development Index is one of the most widely accepted measurements of standard of living. It measures the amount of money a person has and the capacity that person will have for self-improvement based on education and lifespan.[8]

Quality of life. Quality of life refers to how much we enjoy our lives. While having a high standard of living correlates in part to a higher quality of life, the two are not identical. Someone who is quite wealthy may nonetheless not enjoy life as much as a person whose income is below the poverty threshold.

The subjective nature of quality of life makes it difficult to measure, though there are some tools that attempt to do this. One is the World Happiness Report, compiled annually since 2012 by the United Nations Sustainable Development Solutions Network. This study asks respondents around the world to imagine a ladder with ten rungs, with the top (tenth) rung symbolizing their perfect life. They are then asked which rung they are on currently. To see the effect that standard of living has on quality of life, the report correlates the rung number to a variety of UN statistics that measure standard of living for the respondent's country (e.g., national GDP, healthy life expectancy).[9]

The *Global Happiness and Well-Being Policy Report* is an offshoot of the World Happiness Report. Published for the first time in February 2018, it offers specific policy recommendations to governments for improving people's happiness (quality of life) based on governmental approaches to standard of living items.[10]

Another attempt at measuring quality of life is by the Organization for Economic Cooperation and Development (OECD), a forum supported by thirty-seven countries (as of 2021) that recommends "policies that will improve the economic and social well-being of people around the

---

[8] "Human Development Report 2016: Human Development for Everyone" (New York: United Nations Development Program, 2016), 198-201.

[9] "FAQ," World Happiness Report, http://worldhappiness.report/faq/.

[10] *Global Happiness and Well-Being Policy Report*, Global Happiness Council, 2019, https://www.happinesscouncil.org/report/2019/global-happiness-and-well-being-policy-report.

world."[11] The OECD has developed its Better Life Index, which includes eleven data points ranging from standard of living items such as income, health, and education to quality of life items such as happiness, work-life balance, and civic engagement.[12] Recognizing that people value these items differently, the index allows for each item to be weighted to determine how well specific nations would provide a high quality of life for each person. Someone who believes they will have the highest quality of life if they have a greater opportunity to pursue wealth will find a different country more appealing than someone who is primarily concerned with excellent healthcare, for example.

God's promise of abundant life is that people do not need to choose only certain items that will make life more enjoyable. Christ can fulfill us in every way. At the same time, Christians can use tools like the Better Life Index to learn more about the people with whom they seek to share their faith. By knowing what people value in a specific context, Christians are better prepared to work for the common good in a way that is recognized and appreciated as improving quality of life. They also can express their appreciation for people and organizations who are already engaged in this work.

A common way to improve people's happiness is by forging relationships. This commonality sustains across cultures. Christians are especially well-suited to meet this need by providing communities that will give people a sense of value and purpose. We will explore this in detail in the chapter about quality of life.

Eternal life. Eternal life is not something that fits with the secular culture since it is beyond the capacity of humans to verify empirically. Belief in eternal life falls within the pale of religion and requires faith to sustain.

Notwithstanding, the concept of eternal life is essential to how we understand abundant life for several reasons. First, as mentioned above,

---

[11]For more about the OECD, see www.oecd.org/about/.
[12]OECD Better Life Index, www.oecdbetterlifeindex.org/#/11111111111.

without eternal life we miss the full gift of salvation that God offers us. As N. T. Wright explains,

> The work of salvation, in its full sense, is (1) about whole human beings, not merely souls; (2) about the present, not simply the future; and (3) about what God does through us, not merely what God does in and for us. If we can get this straight, we will rediscover the historic basis for the full-orbed mission of the church.[13]

If we let go of the eternal, we relegate the church to being one more humanitarian agency with Christian symbols attached to it. Participating in abundant life means receiving the fullness of life that God offers us, including eternal life, and sharing that with others.

Second, it reminds Christians that we do not believe in an afterlife, but in abundant life. According to Wright, for most people, including Christians, the word *salvation* evokes mental images of an eternal paradise populated by fluffy clouds, winged angels, and golden streets. It refers to what happens to us after we die, saving us from either ceasing to exist or being condemned for our misdeeds.[14]

Jesus teaches that the abundant life he offers is not bifurcated by mortality. We do not experience some of it now and some later, with death standing as a fixed chasm between the two lives. He explained this to Martha when he arrived at Lazarus's tomb.

> Jesus said to her, "Your brother will rise again." Martha said to him, "I know that he will rise again in the resurrection on the last day." Jesus said to her, "I am the resurrection and the life. Those who believe in me, even though they die, will live, and everyone who lives and believes in me will never die." (John 11:23-26 NRSV)

Martha believed that death was an unavoidable reality. Jesus, as the Messiah, had the power to offer life in the physical world (by healing

---

[13]N. T. Wright, *Surprised by Hope: Rethinking Heaven, the Resurrection, and the Mission of the Church* (New York: HarperOne, 2008), 201.

[14]Wright, *Surprised by Hope*, 17-19.

Lazarus before Lazarus died) or life to Lazarus through the resurrection (after Lazarus died), but he could not bridge these two experiences of life. She did not understand that Jesus offered abundant life that overturned death itself. This is what he meant when he responded that whoever lives and believes in him will "never die." Jesus is life, and so long as a person remains in relationship with him, that person's life remains secure. The mortal body may fall away, but the person is neither harmed nor diminished, persisting in God's care. Even the body's physical failing is not final. Jesus proved this by raising Lazarus from the dead. Abundant life overturns death itself so that the mortality of the body is only a temporary state that God easily undoes.

This is the same hope Paul shared when he mused in his letter to the Philippians as to whether he would soon die or remain alive:

> For to me, living is Christ and dying is gain. If I am to live in the flesh, that means fruitful labor for me; and I do not know which I prefer. I am hard pressed between the two: my desire is to depart and be with Christ, for that is far better; but to remain in the flesh is more necessary for you. Since I am convinced of this, I know that I will remain and continue with all of you for your progress and joy in faith. (Philippians 1:21-25 NRSV)

Paul described the hope of participating in abundant life. For him, whether his mortal body was alive or dead, he remained alive in Christ. Physical death is not a factor that can separate him from the abundant life of Christ. Moreover, so long as he was alive in the body, he did not just receive abundant life but participated in it by engaging in the missional work of sharing that life with others. It is this remarkable hope that overflowed from Paul in Romans 8:

> What then are we to say about these things? If God is for us, who is against us? He who did not withhold his own Son, but gave him up for all of us, will he not with him also give us everything else? Who will bring any charge against God's elect? It is God who justifies.

Who is to condemn? It is Christ Jesus, who died, yes, who was raised, who is at the right hand of God, who indeed intercedes for us. Who will separate us from the love of Christ? Will hardship, or distress, or persecution, or famine, or nakedness, or peril, or sword? As it is written,

> "For your sake we are being killed all day long;
>   we are accounted as sheep to be slaughtered."

No, in all these things we are more than conquerors through him who loved us. For I am convinced that neither death, nor life, nor angels, nor rulers, nor things present, nor things to come, nor powers, nor height, nor depth, nor anything else in all creation, will be able to separate us from the love of God in Christ Jesus our Lord. (Romans 8:31-39 NRSV)

Third, while the ironclad hope in eternal life through Jesus Christ may not be something that the secular culture accepts, the problems of fear, death, and meaninglessness are common to all people.[15] There is desperation to find a firm assurance that these problems will not swallow us in the end. Put another way, there is a fervent desire for salvation and the life it brings.

The culture does not shy away from voicing this need for salvation, even if it is eclectic in its articulation and uncertain of what it is seeks. For example, as of August 2021, the website Goodreads listed 8,250 quotations related to salvation from a wide variety of writers, including atheists, new age thinkers, authors of vampire novels, and Christians from across the theological spectrum. In each case, salvation describes something akin to the greatest good that humans can experience, usually in a way that allows us to escape a painful and wearying world.

This escape need not take us out of the world. The *Wall Street Journal* carried an article titled "Technology = Salvation," in which Peter Thiel, the cofounder of PayPal, argued that technological development was the

---

[15]"Death Anxiety," American Psychological Association Dictionary of Psychology, https://dictionary.apa.org/death-anxiety.

key to extricating people from all their problems. "All sorts of things are possible in a world where you have massive progress in technology and related gains in productivity," he said. When technology is developing quickly enough, it can alleviate every potential difficulty. Debt, unemployment, and governmental incompetence are all overcome. This belief in technology rises to the level of a faith for Thiel, such that the only thing he fears is technology not progressing quickly enough to continue lifting society out of the problems that occur. Convinced that this faith is not something he holds alone, he stated, "people don't want to believe that technology is broken."[16]

This muddled desire for salvation is similar to the subjectivity of quality of life. Not all people agree with what they need to be happy, but they all desire to be happy. Likewise, not all agree on what they need to save them from the pressing problems of the world, but they agree that a solution needs to be found that sets things right in perpetuity.

Darrin McMahon demonstrates in *Happiness: A History* that quality of life and eternal life have been linked historically in how Western civilizations sought the purpose of life. From Socrates forward, Western philosophers have determined this purpose is found in attaining some version of salvation, being lifted from the difficulties of life into a greater goodness. If humans could enter this goodness, they would find their chief reason for existence. With the rise of the Enlightenment and modernity, this search began to look more to this world than beyond it for the purpose of life. Spiritual ideas were privatized and minimized as salvation was couched in terms of finding happiness in the here and now. As McMahon put it, the Enlightenment "translated the ultimate question 'How can I be saved' into the pragmatic, 'How can I be happy.'"[17]

Benjamin Franklin stands as an exemplar of this. A precursor to Thiel, he believed that by unraveling the mysteries of how nature operated, people would determine how to decrease the difficulties they faced in

---

[16]Holman W. Jenkins, "Technology = Salvation," *Wall Street Journal*, October 9, 2010.
[17]Darrin M. McMahon, *Happiness: A History* (New York: Grove Press, 2006), 209.

daily life, increase their prosperity, and even attain immortality.[18] He bemoaned that he would not live long enough to see this day, less because it would keep him from having to die and more because he would miss the happy state that humans would enter.

Even with the diminishment of the spiritual, the ongoing need to claim some sort of transcendent happiness shows that the notion of finding a way to live the fullest life possible, freed from danger, is universal to humanity. Regardless of what we believe about ultimate reality, we all recognize that there are great problems facing us and that we need help (whether that help is divine or technological) to overcome these. To reach a place in which we have surmounted these problems will allow us to live in a state of perpetual happiness. This is the greatest good we can achieve, and it will give us hope even when facing death. It would be abundant life.

Regardless of what we believe about how the universe operates, we recognize that we need salvation from the dangers around us, especially from death. The assurance of eternal life provides us with the ultimate hope that we will not succumb to these dangers, because even death cannot hold us. Coupled with the concepts of standard of living and quality of life that are familiar to the secular culture, this hope in eternal life is complemented with concrete and measurable ways of demonstrating how people can experience God's salvation by participating in the abundant life offered through Jesus Christ.

SECULAR CULTURE AS AN OPPORTUNITY

The increasing secularization of the West, as well as other parts of the world, provides an ideal setting for Christians to express their experience of salvation as participating in abundant life. This is because the concept of secularism that has been broadly accepted for centuries is out-of-date and ready to be supplanted.

---

[18]Benjamin Franklin, "Letter to Joseph Priestly," in *The Portable Enlightenment Reader*, ed. Isaac Kramnick (New York: Penguin Books, 1995), 74.

Much of the antireligion bias of secularism is derived from the destruction caused by the Thirty Years' War (1618–1648). A primary motivation for fighting this war was intra-Christian competition. Which form of Christianity (Catholic, Lutheran, or Reformed) would the different regions of Europe officially sanction? The various clergy and lords believed this was a serious enough issue to spill the blood of their subjects for a generation.

The Peace of Westphalia (1648) brought this war to an end in part by privatizing people's religious observance. This allowed everyone to worship according to their conscience without those beliefs interfering with the operations of the state. While this sort of toleration would take centuries to be put into practice, the foundation for it was set here.

According to historian Erin Wilson, defenders of the more hostile forms of secularism have overplayed this moment in history by claiming that religion is always dangerous in the public sphere. Left unchecked, it is wont to promote violence and intolerance. The only safe way to sustain a developed civilization is to privatize religion and let the secular state operate unhindered.[19]

While Wilson legitimately critiques this view of religion, we should not be too quick to dismiss it. It is true that some people used (and continue to use) their religion as justification for engaging in violence. The desire to shape a peace that denied the capacity for this to happen is understandable. Both people of faith and people of no faith can agree on that. Moreover, most of the people who participated in writing and ratifying the Peace of Westphalia were at least professedly Christian, so the agreement was not forced on Christians from the outside.

The ratifiers recognized the death and damage wrought by the misuse of religion and made room through the document for an expanded secular state to avoid that sort of destruction from happening again. This was not kowtowing to secularism but making use of the opportunity

---

[19]Erin K. Wilson, *After Secularism: Rethinking Religion in Global Politics* (New York: Palgrave Macmillan, 2012), 47-49.

secularism offered to help curtail the abuse of power by religion. It was preferable to a solution that restricted religious practice or banned the church from operating. Freedom of conscience and the practice of religion were upheld while the political order focused on serving the tangible common good.

Once again, we live in a time when many people believe that religion is dangerous, especially conservative religion. The onus is on those of us who are people of faith, like the framers of the Peace of Westphalia, to demonstrate that we understand how religion can be misused. However, instead of doing this by dialing back the engagement of the church in the public square, the desperation of the present day calls for us to demonstrate how the church should be more engaged for the common good.

If we can show that we are concerned for the well-being of other people not because we are seeking cultural or institutional dominance but because working for the common good is a facet of participating in the abundant life offered through Christ, we can open a new door of engagement with the culture. By celebrating and working alongside people of goodwill who are already committed to the common good of improving the standard of living and quality of life of those in need, we can find ways of building credibility even in a secular context.[20] This will allow us to share about eternal life as welcome participants in promoting

---

[20]I emphasize the notion of "people of goodwill" because there will always be some people who remain resistant to any notion of salvation, secular or otherwise. Taylor expands on this point, suggesting that there are three parties in the current Western culture who debate the nature of humanity: secular humanists, neo-Nietzscheans, and those who acknowledge some good beyond life (with Christians falling into the last group). He contends that it is possible for each group to align with one of the others at some point. The neo-Nietzscheans and the religious both point to the failed efforts that secular humanism alone can bring about; the secular humanists and the religious deplore the violence and will-to-power espoused by the neo-Nietzscheans; and the neo-Nietzscheans and the secular humanists consider the transcendent claims of the religious to be out-of-step with human nature. I am not suggesting that this idea of abundant life can completely undercut the fundamental disagreements among these groups. I do contend, however, that it can provide a stronger bridge between Christians and those in the other two parties on the points where they already agree: the neo-Nietzscheans by engaging with the secular powers and authorities of the world in measurable ways, the secular humanists by demonstrating a clear and compelling case for working toward the common good. Insofar as it can accomplish this, it will establish a much stronger witness to all groups that otherwise are caught in the immanent frame that would close their worldview to faith. Of course, this witness will only be meaningful for those

the common good rather than as suspicious interlopers in the public square. Clarifying our experience of salvation as participating in abundant life provides us the intellectual framework and practical impetus for doing this.

THEOLOGICAL, BIBLICAL, AND PRACTICAL

The balance of the book will be spent building the case for articulating the Christian experience of salvation as participating in abundant life. The opening chapters will lay the internal Christian framework for this. Chapter two will reflect on how different theological traditions can not only maintain their integrity but be enriched by accepting this way of articulating the Christian experience of salvation. Chapter three will provide an overview of biblical teaching about salvation. It will demonstrate that when looking at the whole salvation narrative across the Hebrew Scriptures and the New Testament, the concept of salvation is holistic, entailing God rescuing us from dangers in this world and the next.

The later chapters will look at how this framework intersects with secular ways of thinking about life and working to improve it. In chapters four and five we will treat the concepts of standard of living and quality of life, respectively. In these chapters we will draw heavily from secular organizations that deal with these ideas and look at how Christians can connect with them and critique them in light of the full offer of abundant life through Christ. We will especially consider how people of goodwill, regardless of their faith, can work together to improve people's standard of living and quality of life.

Chapter six will address eternal life. In it we will consider what it means for Christians to steward the gospel message, especially the call to invite people to receive forgiveness and eternal life so they can be saved from divine judgment, in an otherwise secular setting. To do this, we will draw from missionaries Lesslie Newbigin and E. Stanley Jones.

---

who have the goodwill both to desire good for their neighbor and to see that Christians are capable of likewise desiring this in measurable ways. Taylor, *A Secular Age*, 636-37.

Finally, the conclusion will remind us that looking to God for abundant life in both this world and the next has deep roots in the church by reflecting on the Divine Liturgy. Although applying the terminology of standard of living and quality of life to Christian salvation is new, the notion of doing this alongside eternal life is ancient. Our move to express salvation in this way is less an innovation than a reclamation of the living Christian tradition.

The appendix provides a reflection on metrics Christians can use to determine how fully they are participating in abundant life along with individual and congregational scorecards for tracking this. The scorecards are not to determine whether someone is saved! Salvation comes through grace alone (Ephesians 2:8-9). Rather, they suggest ways Christians can hold themselves accountable for both receiving the gifts God has given them and deploying those gifts to make an impact in the world around them. And since many congregations and denominations prefer quantifiable data because it is easier to collect, interpret, and summarize, these scorecards rely heavily on numbers.

My prayer for this book is that it (1) helps Christians better articulate their beliefs, especially about ultimate things that motivate their ministries, and (2) equips Christians to live out their salvation in the world as it is, learning how they can maneuver in a secular culture without feeling embattled or as if they must trade off the fullness of their faith to be effective. In doing both these things, I believe that Christians will be more like Jesus.

I also pray that it will give us a way to talk about and enact salvation today that will be meaningful and attractive to those who live around us. It will be a way that commends rather than condemns the secular world's desire to bring a better life to all people and that serves as a signpost that shows both a better standard of living and a better quality of life flow out of the abundant life that is offered by God through Jesus Christ.

2

Experiencing Salvation

But someone will ask, "How are the dead raised?
With what kind of body will they come?"

1 CORINTHIANS 15:35

AFTER AFFIRMING CHRIST'S RESURRECTION in the first half of
1 Corinthians 15, Paul entertained the above question. It is likely he had
encountered this question before as a challenge to his belief in the resurrection. It could be read as something like, "There is an obvious flaw in
your logic, Paul. Surely you agree that a physical body decays after death.
Given this irrefutable fact, how can there be a resurrection from death?
The original physical body is no longer capable of being raised!" Paul was
not impressed with this line of reasoning, given that he prefaced his response with the words "How foolish!"

Despite his disdain for the question, Paul answered it, explaining that
the resurrected body would not have the same attributes as the mortal
body, so it would not be subject to decay. He wrote, "This perishable body
must put on imperishability, and this mortal body must put on immortality" (1 Corinthians 15:53 NRSV).

But why answer if he thought the question was so ludicrous?

One reason would be to provide an apologetic for Christians.
This was likely a common challenge that Christians faced, and they
needed direction on how to answer it. Paul's response equipped his

readers to explain the fallacy of the argument being made against the resurrection.

In addition, he likely realized that well-meaning Christians were asking a similar question for a different reason. What will it be like to enter fully into salvation when death itself is destroyed and all the forces of evil are overcome? This was not meant to challenge the resurrection but to understand what experiencing it would be like.

The epistle of 1 John also hints at Christian curiosity about experiencing salvation. It declares, "Beloved, we are God's children now; what we will be has not yet been revealed. What we do know is this: when he is revealed, we will be like him, for we will see him as he is" (1 John 3:2 NRSV). The author acknowledged that the future is a mystery but assured his readers that it would be good and that it would build on their current experiences of God's goodness.

These questions are not confined to the first century AD. The contemporary Christian music band Mercy Me released the song "I Can Only Imagine" in 1999. In it, the band ponders what it will be like to live in the final state of glory. In one verse they muse,

> I can only imagine what it will be like
> When I walk, by your side
> I can only imagine what my eyes will see
> When your face is before me
> I can only imagine
> I can only imagine[1]

These questions, whether asked in the earliest days of Christianity or now, address salvation experientially. They ask what it is like to perceive salvation from the inside—as those who are already saved from harm and participating in the glory of God.

This book picks up on this line of questions. It asks what it is like to experience salvation as a Christian. The answer it gives is that we

---

[1]"I Can Only Imagine," track 5 on Mercy Me, *The Worship Project*, self-released, 1999.

experience salvation by participating in abundant life. This participation is not just something we experience ultimately, though. We
begin to participate in the abundant life offered by God through Jesus
Christ now as we receive God's provisions in this world and as we begin
to join God in mission by sharing those provisions with others. More
than this, even those who are not Christian participate in a portion of
this abundant life because they too are receiving good gifts in this life
and may be sharing those gifts with others, especially through working
to improve people's standard of living and quality of life. Christians
should not minimize how God is already moving in these people but
should come alongside them to complete their participation in
abundant life by sharing the gospel message about eternal life
through Christ.[2]

Christians, however, are not a monolithic group. There are multiple
theological traditions, each with emphases on how it understands God
and God's activity. For the idea of participating in abundant life to be
useful, it must allow for Christians from different theological traditions
to maintain their integrity while still making use of it. It should also
enrich these traditions.

KEEPING THE INTEGRITY OF THEOLOGICAL TRADITIONS

Systematic theology asks three core questions: Who is God? What does
God do? How should we respond to God based on who God is and what
God does? Related to salvation, these questions ask about the nature of

---

[2]While I approach this from the perspective of Christian witness rather than cultural analysis, using
the approach of experience is similar to what Charles Taylor sought to do in *A Secular Age*. He wrote
in his introduction, "I want to talk about belief and unbelief, not as rival *theories*, that is, ways that
people account for existence, or morality, whether by God or something else in nature, or whatever.
Rather, what I want to do is focus attention on the different kinds of lived experience involved
in understanding your life in one way or the other, on what it's like to live as a believer or an
unbeliever. . . . Somewhere, in some activity, or condition, lies a fullness, a richness; that is, in that
place (activity or condition), life is fuller, richer, deeper, more worthwhile, more admirable, more
what it should be." Taylor, *A Secular Age*, 4-5. I agree with Taylor that there is some level of fullness
in the life of all people regardless of their faith. My project is to present the Christian experience of
participating in abundant life as the most fulfilling of these experiences, as it meets the deepest
desires and highest aspirations of humanity.

the God who offers us salvation, the ways in which God operates to make salvation possible, and how we are to respond so we can receive this salvation.

The nature of God and what God does are closely related when dealing with salvation. This is because all Christians agree that God offers salvation through Jesus Christ. The question is how God works through Jesus to provide this salvation. This is a point of significant contention. A brief overview of three theological traditions demonstrates this.

Eastern Orthodox Christians emphasize God's holiness and the need for humans to be healed of their sinful nature so they can enter a perfect state of holy communion with the triune God (a process known as *theosis*). God provides for this through the incarnation of the second person of the Trinity as Jesus of Nazareth. Through the incarnation, God heals humanity from its sin sickness and prepares it for holiness. Irenaeus articulated this: "The Word of God, our Lord Jesus Christ, who did, through His transcendent love, become what we are, that He might bring us to be even what He is Himself."[3]

Reformed theology claims that, in addition to being holy, God's primary attribute is being sovereign over all things. One result of this is that God sovereignly elects who will share in God's glory for eternity.[4] However, there is a problem. Even though God has elected these people, they carry the original sin of Adam and therefore have offended the holiness of God. This means that God must refuse them access to God's glory. To make the elect worthy, they must be purged of their sin and made holy. God sent Jesus to do both these things. By living a sinless life yet accepting death on the cross, Jesus substituted himself in place of the elect and satisfied the need for God to punish sin. In doing this, Jesus also

---

[3]Irenaeus, preface to "Against Heresies, Book V," in *The Apostolic Fathers with Justin Martyr and Irenaeus*, ed. Alexander Roberts and James Donaldson, rev. A. Cleveland Coxe, vol. 1 of *Ante-Nicene Fathers* (Peabody, MA: Hendrickson Publishers, 2004), 526.

[4]John Calvin, *Calvin: Institutes of the Christian Religion*, trans. Ford Lewis Battles, ed. John T. McNeill, The Library of Christian Classics (Philadelphia: The Westminster Press, 1960), 921 §3.21.1.

transferred his holiness to the elect so that God could accept them into glory.[5]

Wesleyan/Arminian theology points to holiness and graciousness as God's chief attributes, creating something of a hybrid between Orthodox and Reformed views of salvation. It agrees that God is holy and that humans must be saved from their sin to share in that holiness. At the same time, it contends that God expects humans to participate in the process of becoming holy, meaning that people are free to choose whether they will participate in God's salvation. As such, God sends Jesus to atone for all humanity's sins as well as to demonstrate what leading a holy life looks like. As an act of grace, God also sends the Holy Spirit to empower all people to accept the truth of Christ's atonement and to begin living in a holy way.[6]

Each of these examples necessitates slightly different ways for people to respond to God in order to participate in the salvation that God offers. For the Orthodox, the ideal response is to commit to a monastic life, or at least a life that is defined by Orthodox traditions and rituals, to shut out the corruption of the world and draw ever closer to the holiness of God. For the Reformed, the elect are called to believe the truth of what God has done through Jesus Christ and to accept their partici-pation in God's salvation gratefully. For the Wesleyan/Arminians, people must awaken to the truth of what God has provided through Jesus Christ and cooperate with the grace God has given them so they can lead holy lives.

These different theological perspectives also lead to different answers for the experiential questions. Orthodox Christians experience salvation chiefly in the church. The communion among the faithful, the saints, and

---

[5]Calvin expounds on this in his *Institutes of the Christian Religion*, which explains the effect of Adam's sin on humanity (Book 2, Chapter 1) and how Jesus serves as a sacrifice in place of humanity to provide salvation (Book 2, Chapter 12.3 and Book 2, Chapter 16.5-7).

[6]John Wesley is the best-known expositor of this view of salvation, most notably in his sermon "The Scripture Way of Salvation," in which he contended that God's saving grace awakens, justifies, and sanctifies. John Wesley, Sermon 43, "The Scripture Way of Salvation," in *Sermons II*, ed. Albert C. Outler, vol. 2 of *The Bicentennial Edition of the Works of John Wesley* (Nashville: Abingdon Press, 1976–).

Jesus Christ prepares them for being in communion with the Holy Trinity in glory. For the Reformed, the elect stand as those who are forgiven, seek to obey the commands of God as revealed in the Scripture, and await the full consummation of this when they stand before the throne of judgment from which God will declare them to be holy because of the atoning work of Jesus Christ. For the Wesleyan/Arminians, salvation is a process of being transformed by the grace of God through faith with the hope of attaining complete sanctification in this life and of one day being glorified. It also requires an intertwining of the Christian's salvation and the salvation of others. The universal grace of God calls them to become agents of that grace, sharing it through word and deed so that others might experience God's goodness in this life and claim God's gracious gift of salvation through Jesus Christ as well. This includes both personal acts of piety and social engagement.

These are brief and overly general presentations of these three theological traditions. Each can be nuanced substantially. For example, the Orthodox and Reformed believe in the need to love their neighbors and find value in social engagement. The Reformed and Wesleyan/Arminians do not deny the importance of the church. The Wesleyan/Arminians and the Orthodox agree that God has freedom to act apart from human agency. While each has its emphasis, all of them recognize a holistic work of God that extends through creation into eternity. God is good and takes the initiative through Jesus Christ to rescue people from dangers that are too big for them so they can securely share in God's goodness. In doing this, God invites people into abundant life.

This opens the door for each tradition to claim the idea that Christian salvation is experienced as participating in abundant life without the tradition impugning its uniqueness. The Orthodox can understand participating in the abundant life of God as Christians living in faithful communion with God such that the uncreated light of God infuses their nature and shines out to others. The Reformed can explain participating in the abundant life of God as being obedient to the moral commandments revealed in Scripture in a way that honors the grace God has given them for eternity. The Wesleyan/Arminian can see participating in abundant life as the outworking of salvation in this life as the image of God is restored in their character. The differentiation among the theological traditions is not about *if* God wants people to experience abundant life in this world and the next but *how* God makes participating in abundant life possible.

On a practical level, participating in abundant life as an experience of salvation leads to the same activity by all Christians regardless of theological tradition: they will love God and neighbor. They will love God by receiving the good gifts God offers them in this life, rendering thanks and praise in return for the provision God makes in this world, and looking with hope and anticipation to an eternity in glory with the God they love. They will also love their neighbor by following the example and the commandments of Christ in how they treat other people. This will especially involve sharing the good gifts God has given them with the needy, whether they need physical, social, psychological, spiritual, or any other kind of aid. And, as they are loving God and neighbor, they will recognize that they are being saved from the corruption of this world and prepared for the next in an ongoing way.

ENRICHING THE THEOLOGICAL TRADITIONS

The idea of experiencing salvation as participating in abundant life does more than fit with different theological traditions; it enriches them in two ways. First, it calls on the traditions to avoid minimizing their understanding of salvation by reducing it to only human experience or by making it into a prosperity gospel. Second, it provides a conceptual framework that helps bridge rifts within the church and between the church and the world.

Avoiding a minimized salvation. The heart of Christian teaching about salvation is that it is rooted in God's engagement with human history. If God did not choose to enter human history, then salvation would not be available. The biblical narrative is essentially the story of this divine activity.

God begins by creating all things. This includes Adam and Eve, whom God places in the paradise of the Garden of Eden to share in the fullness of life. However, humanity rejects God's gift of life by sinning and so bringing death to the world (Genesis 2:17). To avoid humanity and the rest of creation succumbing to death, God intervenes many times throughout the ensuing millennia to make life available again. This often takes the form of sustaining life in physical ways. God chooses Abram, renaming him Abraham, and blesses him to become a blessing to all nations by becoming the progenitor of the Hebrew people. God later sends Moses to save the Hebrews and lead them to the Promised Land. God raises up David to become the king of Israel and to save the Israelites from the nations that had sought to harm them. Crowning all of this, God becomes incarnate in the person of Jesus of Nazareth. Every aspect of Jesus' life and ministry carried salvific importance, culminating in his suffering, death, and resurrection to save people from sin and death.

There are four important points tied to salvation being rooted in God's engagement in human history. First, while salvation is experienced by humans, it cannot be reduced to subjective human experience. This is why N. T. Wright states that the gospel is good news, not just good advice.[7] It is good because it announces that God cares about our human struggles and limitations, especially the evils and problems that we cannot overcome ourselves. It is supremely good because God cares enough to overcome these problems for us and create a way for life to continue unhindered. It is news because God did this in our midst, using means that humans can see, recognize, grasp, and sometimes even measure. God did not just make a decision in heaven but worked out our salvation on earth with implications for this life and the next.

---

[7]N. T. Wright, *Simply Good News: Why the Gospel Is News and What Makes It Good* (New York: HarperOne, 2015), 5.

Second, salvation is initiated by God. God entered human history and began providing life to humans before we could even recognize our need for that life. God created Adam and Eve and set them in Paradise—initiating human existence in a way that provided abundant life from the beginning. God chose Abram before Abram called on God or possibly even believed in God, granting him an abundance of life through his multitude of progeny and saving him from a life of childless obscurity. God saved Moses from the river as an infant and endowed him with the gift to lead people out of slavery into an abundant land. God saved David as a child from the predators who attacked his father's sheep, giving him the charism of leadership to save the people of Israel from their enemies so they could enjoy abundant blessings as a nation. God sent Jesus to save us all from sin and death, promising us abundant life in this world and the next. In each case, the recipients of God's abundant life did nothing to earn God's work on their behalf. God began the process of salvation apart from human activity, defining it and its scope.

Third, the salvific work of God through Jesus Christ is cosmic in nature. It is not just about providing abundant life to individuals but about re-shaping the universe itself. In his suffering and death, Jesus encountered every aspect of evil that humans and the powers of darkness could devise, and he rose victoriously over them to obliterate evil and death. He renewed all of creation in the resurrection. To receive abundant life, then, is not a matter of just feeling better about ourselves or enjoying our lives more. Rather, it is a matter of organizing our lives around the new, gracious order of the universe. This new order is life-giving, and that life radiates through this world and into eternity.

This leads to the fourth point, that receiving salvation prompts people into mission. God initially placed Adam and Eve in Paradise that they might carry out the mission of stewarding and filling creation. God chose Abram so that he could become a father to a nation. God saved Moses and David so they could lead others into God's greater blessings through the covenant. God sent Jesus so he could give his life as a ransom for many and offer abundant life as the firstborn of a new creation. When God invites us to receive abundant life, God also invites us to participate in God's redemptive purposes for the world. God sends us in mission.[8]

This idea of a God-initiated, cosmic, missional experience of salvation protects theological traditions from minimizing the Christian experience of salvation. It is not just about how individuals relate to God but about how humans are drawn into the metanarrative of God's salvific work in the world. This work involves pouring forth life to all creation and inviting people to participate in that life by receiving it and sharing it with others in ways that are objectively tangible and measurable.

Abundant life with enjoyment and suffering. Even with this explanation of how participating in abundant life prompts us into mission, the language used to describe aspects of abundant life may still be problematic. Both *standard of living* and *quality of life* are terms drawn from economics, a point that we will explore in greater detail in the chapters dedicated to each concept. By using these terms there is a potential for devolving the idea of participating in abundant life into a crass prosperity gospel, promising health and wealth in this world and an escape to the mansions of heaven in the next.

Kate Bowler, a church historian and ethnographer who has studied the prosperity gospel in the United States, defines the prosperity gospel this way:

> The prosperity gospel . . . centers around four themes: *faith, wealth, health,* and *victory.* (1) It conceives of *faith* as an activator, a power that unleashes spiritual forces and turns the spoken word into reality. (2) The movement depicts faith as palpably demonstrated

---

[8]The idea that God sends the church in mission is accepted by all Christians. However, what that sending looks like and how it relates specifically to God and God's purposes are points of debate among missiologists. See especially Craig Ott, ed., *The Mission of the Church: Five Views in Conversation* (Grand Rapids, MI: Baker Academic, 2016) for insights from multiple perspectives on this point. In this text, I do not advocate for one of these perspectives over another so much as argue that we would do better to harmonize them to provide as wide a vision as possible of God's salvation and the goodness God purposes for us.

in *wealth* and (3) *health*. It can be measured in both the wallet (one's personal wealth) and in the body (one's personal health), making material reality the measure of the success of immaterial faith. (4) The movement expects faith to be marked by *victory*. . . . All four hallmarks emphasize demonstrable results, a faith that may be calculated by the outcome of a successful life.[9]

There are points of agreement between the idea of participating in abundant life and what the prosperity gospel teaches. God does bless people with health, wealth, and other good things in this world. One of the signs of God's validation of the patriarchs and the kings of Israel was the wealth they accrued and the long, vital lives God granted those who remained faithful.

These blessings were not reserved for only the elite. Throughout the Bible God provides a variety of blessings that improve people's standard of living and quality of life. God sends power to heal people of all manner of diseases, even raising them from death and restoring them to bodily wholeness; makes food available for hungry people to eat and water for thirsty people to drink; and even sends a fish with money inside its mouth to pay the temple tax for Simon Peter and Jesus. These gifts were not always just to help people in dire need either. Jesus' first miracle was turning water into ample amounts of wine even after the people at the party had drunk quite a bit.

The question is not whether God is willing to provide more than we need to survive or if God wants us to enjoy life. God does. The question is whether our lives should be ordered around receiving and consuming these good things. The answer is no.

Using economic terms is not meant to reduce salvation but to explain the present experience of God's salvation—that it deals with the real struggles people face in this world related to money and health—in a way

---

[9]Kate Bowler, *Blessed: A History of the American Prosperity Gospel* (New York: Oxford University Press, 2013), 7.

that makes sense in a secular culture. It also provides concrete evidence of the abundance God provides for those who seek God. The goal of this is not to have people fixate on the blessings themselves but to recognize God as the source. God not only guarantees that mortal death is not the end of life but also cares about how we live in this world. God wants us to both live eternally and live well.

Theological traditions would be enriched if they accepted and articulated this. The seductive nature of worldly wealth, health, and pleasure often make Christian theologies uncomfortable with acknowledging that God wants us to enjoy our lives. Yet the biblical witness is clear about this. To deny it is to minimize the abundance that God desires to share with us.

At the same time, our ability to claim the blessings God desires us to have in this world must be set within the cosmic-sized, missional salvation God has unfolded through human history. This means being willing to accept suffering as disciples of Jesus.

It is clear from the Bible that becoming a disciple of Jesus includes suffering. This suffering is not a result of any failure or wrongdoing. Rather, it is frequently experienced by the most faithful disciples and is seen as a reason to rejoice because it means God has deemed the disciple worthy to suffer just as Jesus did (1 Peter 4:12-13). As Alan Hirsch and Mark Nelson write, "Life to the full involves both death *and* life, both crucifixion *and* resurrection. The safe, secure, and prosperous life is *not* the life the followers of Jesus have been given and are called to participate in."[10] God desires us to enjoy all the benefits of abundant life, but the missional call that allows us to participate in that abundant life is never undercut by this enjoyment.

The idea that being a disciple of Jesus Christ entails suffering makes sense only if we believe in a cosmic salvation rather than a prosperity gospel. A cosmic salvation assures us that we are already held fast in the care of God. This means that even if we have everything taken from us,

---

[10]Alan Hirsch and Mark Nelson, *Reframation: Seeing God, People, and Mission Through Reenchanted Frames* (Los Angeles: 100 Movements Publishing, 2019), 88.

we are assured that our life is in no way diminished. As Paul explains, "For all things are yours, whether . . . the world or life or death or the present or the future—all belong to you, and you belong to Christ, and Christ belongs to God" (1 Corinthians 3:21-23 NRSV). It also means we are free to give away the blessings we receive to benefit others because we know we will never lack for God's abundant life. As Jesus exhorted the disciples, "Freely you have received; freely give" (Matthew 10:8).

This does not mean that having our wealth, health, or other earthly blessings taken away is easy or painless. The Bible acknowledges this, especially in the anguish experienced by Job. Even Jesus openly expressed his pain when he gave himself to be tortured and crucified. We should not minimize or ignore this lest we treat those who suffer unlovingly.

At the same time, our assurance of God's abundant life also means that we can count whatever struggles we face as only a "slight momentary affliction" (2 Corinthians 4:17 NRSV) and "not worth comparing with the glory about to be revealed to us" (Romans 8:18 NRSV). The abundant life we participate in allows us both to accept suffering as part of God's work in our lives and trust that suffering will be overcome fully when God sets all things right.

If all God desires is for us to enjoy life, the call to discipleship that includes suffering makes no sense. Only Christians who were not faithful enough to receive God's victory would suffer. This is what the prosperity gospel teaches, blaming the individual who is suffering for having a lack of faith, which compounds the misery they experience.[11]

The prosperity gospel also undercuts the missional requirement of participating in abundant life. If we believe that God will bless anyone with abundance if they have sufficient faith, we should not help others who have physical needs beyond exhorting them to have faith so they can be blessed. Our helping them beyond this would minimize their ability to know God's victory for themselves.

---

[11]Hirsch and Nelson, *Reframation*, 150-52.

The prosperity gospel is a warped understanding of what it means to love God and love neighbor, which means that it diverges from what we mean by participating in abundant life. It teaches that we do not order our lives according to Christ's teaching, but Christ orders his blessings to support and fulfill our comfort. This shrinks our understanding of salvation to include only what is enjoyable for us. Those who are outside the Christian faith are taught that Christians do not care about the common good, only about themselves. This vitiates the Christian witness to the world. Participating in abundant life rejects all of this.

A cosmic salvation. Participating in abundant life enriches theological traditions by pointing toward the cosmic nature of salvation. This allows Christians both to receive the good gifts God offers in this world and to accept suffering as a potential (and even likely) attendant to serving God. Set free from worrying about whether we will have enough or if we will be able to bear any suffering we may undergo, the most faithful activity Christians can engage in is to reach out in love toward God and neighbor. This includes improving people's standard of living and quality of life as well as sharing the gospel with them so they can come to faith in Jesus Christ and claim the fullness of life.

The economic terms therefore do not reduce our understanding of God's abundant life. Rather, the logic of participating in abundant life transfigures the terms *standard of living* and *quality of life* and places them at the service of the cosmic transformation God brings through Christ. In doing this, we follow the advice of St. Gregory Palamas on how theology may profitably engage with secular philosophy:

> Is there then anything of use in this philosophy? Certainly; for just as there is much therapeutic value even in substances obtained from the flesh of serpents, and the doctors consider there is no better and more useful medicine than that derived from this source, so there is something of benefit to be had even from the profane philosophers—but somewhat as in a mixture of honey and hemlock.

So it is most needful that those who wish to separate out the honey
from the mixture should beware that they do not take the deadly
residue by mistake.[12]

Bridges for theological engagement. Presenting the Christian experience of salvation as participating in abundant life not only enriches
theological traditions by steering them away from reduced and faulty
soteriologies; it opens the door for them to expand their witness. It does
this by providing a common language that facilitates engagements within
the global church and with the larger culture. Within the church, it gives
greater voice to Majority World Christians, providing them an equal
place to express their experiences of the Christian faith. With the larger
culture, it offers new means to be credible outside of the church, including through new language to talk about salvation, new metrics to
show that God cares about the common good, and new guidelines for
public engagement.

Normalizing the Majority World Christian experience. The term
Majority World refers to those nations outside of what is often referred to
as "the West," meaning western European nations and nations that pre-
dominantly remain settled by people of western European origin, such as
the United States, Canada, Australia, and New Zealand. The word *majority* is used because these nations make up the preponderance of the
global population. They also contain the majority of the global Christian
population. Using the term *Majority World* reminds those of us in the
West that we may have more resources and geopolitical influence, but we
are not the majority and our experience of the Christian faith is not nor-
mative for most Christians worldwide.

Unlike the West, the Majority World's intellectual development was
not forged out of the Enlightenment. This means the secular forces of
rationalism and empiricism never defined it in the same way that they
defined the West. The result is that many Majority World nations are

---

[12]St. Gregory Palamas, *The Triads* (New York: Paulist Press, 1983), 28.

more open to the notion of the spirit world and supernatural. At the same time, because the Majority World tends to be impoverished compared to the West, Christians in the Majority World take God's physical provision in this world more seriously.

These differences come out in how Majority World scholars discuss salvation. For example, Emily J. Choge-Kerama, an African theologian, suggests that the minimized ways the Western churches have come to understand salvation neglects the needs that African people have. This is especially disappointing because she believes that

> when missionaries came to Africa they did not divide the temporal and the sacred. They did not just emphasize preaching the gospel and saving souls. . . . Evangelism came at the same time as the establishment of mission schools, hospitals, and farming stations. . . . Missionaries knew they had to minister to the whole person, but today that holistic aspect is not seen.[13]

To reclaim this holistic view of salvation, Kerama argues that Christians must consider the realities facing many Africans today. To do this, she suggests that any discussion of salvation should include the following:

1. Proclaiming "the lordship of Jesus Christ over powers and principalities." This includes giving people hope that they are protected from "all sorts of enemies, including spirits and sorcerers [as well as] political power that allows rampant corruption, nepotism, and various forms of social injustice."[14]

2. Providing a community that transcends ethnic and national barriers. This would "counteract the negative narratives of individualism, the neglect of vulnerable children and youth, and even care for the stranger in the face of terrorist activities."[15]

---

[13]Emily J. Choge-Kerama, "Telling Our Stories: Salvation in the African Context," in *Majority World Theology: Christian Doctrine in Global Context*, ed. Gene L. Green, Stephen T. Pardue, and K. K. Yeo (Downers Grove, IL: IVP Academic, 2020), 386.

[14]Choge-Kerama, "Telling Our Stories," 387-88.

[15]Choge-Kerama, "Telling Our Stories," 388.

3. Fostering hospitality in a way "that the efforts of the stranger and
   the host are combined to make provision for the community. It is
   not just one-sided. All work together for the good of the community. It means that even as Christians live in their communities,
   they will make a difference like the early Christians made."[16]

Fellow African scholar Rosinah Mmannana Gabaitse makes a similar
point. Drawing on Luke 4, in which Jesus announced his ministry in the
synagogue by declaring he had come to proclaim good news to the poor,
freedom to the prisoners, recovery of sight to the blind, and to set the
oppressed free, she states,

> The existence of the unfavorable conditions described in
> Luke 4:18-19 is real and these conditions prevent human beings,
> both men and women, from experiencing complete salvation. The
> oppression described in Luke 4:18-19 can be imposed on people by
> political, sociocultural, and economic systems.[17]

The language of both scholars, which emphasizes the experience of God's
provision in this life, would be welcomed and buttressed by articulating
the Christian experience of salvation as participating in abundant life,
with abundant life explicated in terms of standard of living, quality of life,
and eternal life. Not only would a wider adoption of this explanation of
abundant life give African Christians a more central place in forging
Christian theology and ministry practices worldwide, it would allow
Western and African Christians a beneficial foundation for engaging in
ministry as equals rather than in a benefactor-client relationship driven
by who controls financial means.

A similar situation would be possible with Latin Americans. Jules A.
Martinez-Olivieri contends that Latin Americans resist the idea of transcultural theologies, preferring theology that is formed in a cultural

---

[16]Choge-Kerama, "Telling Our Stories," 389.
[17]Rosinah Mmannana Gabaitse, "Luke 4:18-19 and Salvation: Marginalization of Women in the
Pentecostal Church in Botswana," in Green, Pardue, and Yeo, *Majority World Theology*, 400.

context.[18] This is because such transcultural theologies have often ignored the lived experiences of Latin America, in which an Indigenous Christian theology "presents itself as an attempt to take on the question of how to discern God's presence in a situation of destitution and human turmoil."[19] The reduced views of salvation from "the West" have not resonated with this.

It is out of their context that many Latin Americans have come to understand salvation as liberation. Martinez-Olivieri explains that "liberation is a soteriological concept that attempts to capture the historical experience of divine redemptive acts."[20] Drawing from Gustavo Gutiérrez, he offers three levels of salvation as understood through the lens of liberation: (1) sociopolitical, which liberates the marginalized and oppressed; (2) anthropological, which provides a community of equals for all people; and (3) theological, which forgives sin and allows for a renewal of relationships between all people and God.[21]

Martinez-Olivieri insists that all three aspects of salvation must be maintained for liberation to occur. God enters the temporal affairs of humanity to save people from immediate physical, social, political, and economic needs as well as to provide the "metaphysical aspects of Christ's actions" through conquering sin.[22] The temporal and metaphysical are linked because only in recognizing how Christ overthrows sin can Christians hope for the final overcoming of evil and oppression in the world.

There is resonance between the Latin American notion of salvation as liberation and the idea of experiencing salvation as participating in abundant life. The abundant life God gives us through Christ saves us from problems in this world, including the situations that create poverty and marginalization; establishes us with dignity in communities of faith;

---

[18]Jules A. Martinez-Olivieri, "*Con Las Venas Abiertas*: The Hope of Life and Salvation in Latin American Theologies," in Green, Pardue, and Yeo, *Majority World Theology*, 405-6.

[19]Martinez-Olivieri, "*Con Las Venas Abiertas*," 405.

[20]Martinez-Olivieri, "*Con Las Venas Abiertas*," 406.

[21]Martinez-Olivieri, "*Con Las Venas Abiertas*," 406.

[22]Martinez-Olivieri, "*Con Las Venas Abiertas*," 413.

and points us to the ultimate salvation of God in eternal glory. By not just receiving, but participating, in abundant life, we experience liberation as those who are freed both from want and from self-centeredness. We give freely of ourselves and our God-provided resources to support justice for our neighbors.

A similar point is made by Ray Aldred, who is a member of the First Nations in Canada. He argues that salvation could be experienced in part through reconciliation between Indigenous peoples and the peoples who colonized their lands. "Healing and restored relationship is a legitimate goal for all who call the land of Canada home," he writes.[23] This sort of reconciliation offers both the Indigenous people and the descendants of the colonizers the ability to come together by setting the Indigenous people free from the self-hatred they have long experienced and by creating a way for descendants of the colonizers to recognize and rebuild what they destroyed as their ancestors took root in the land.

Aldred suggests that this understanding of salvation is something that makes sense whether people are Christian or not:

> Repentance, as seen as a contrite sorrow for sin and a turning to a new way of life, is understandable in a Canadian context by both indigenous and Christian people. It is then possible to see Christian repentance and salvation as a fulfillment of the harmony hoped for by indigenous spirituality.[24]

This point supports the idea that explaining the Christian experience of salvation as abundant life creates the opportunity for Christians to work for the common good alongside others regardless of their faith. Christians can even spearhead these efforts. People may not be awakened to follow Jesus Christ by the call to turn from sin or to seek glory after death, but they can recognize when people are harmed in this world and often are

---

[23]Ray Aldred, "An Indigenous Reinterpretation of Repentance: A Step on the Journey to Reconciliation," in Green, Pardue, and Yeo, *Majority World Theology*, 442.

[24]Aldred, "Indigenous Reinterpretation of Repentance," 443.

open to invitations to help make those things right.[25] It would be even more powerful if Christians from marginalized social, ethnic, or other groups were to take the lead in this work. This would demonstrate that the work of reconciliation had already begun in the church. Christians would show themselves to be those who had found not only healing through Christ but purpose and power to offer that healing to others.

Theological traditions would be enriched by making room for the voices and practices of the Majority World. Inviting this conversation would be difficult at times, stretching the categories and assumptions that especially the Western traditions have maintained for centuries. However, this stretching itself would help Christians participate more fully in the abundant life of Christ. By decentering culturally specific experiences of salvation that are often the controlling narrative for shaping theological traditions and replacing them with the multivalent experiences of salvation that arise from listening to Christians across the globe, each tradition would have a richer understanding of abundant life to express in their respective soteriologies.

New language. The problem of religious language is well-known in philosophy and theology. How can we as Christians speak about God in a meaningful way since God is, by our own admission, impossible for us to understand or describe given our limited human faculties? The theological traditions within Christianity have appealed to the doctrine of revelation to answer this question, explaining that our capacity to speak about God is grounded in God first reaching out to us in a way that we can understand. By basing our language about God on this revelation, we

---

[25]Rick Richardson, director of the Billy Graham Research Institute, found in a survey of two thousand unchurched people in the United States that sixty-two percent of unchurched people said that they would accept an invitation to a church-sponsored event focused on making their neighborhood safer. Richardson points out that hosting such an event would both demonstrate the church's concern for the common good in a way people could appreciate and open the door for further evangelism. "Of course, we don't just sponsor such events to get points and bring unchurched people to the church. We sponsor events on safety because we care about neighbors and we care about safety. Having unchurched people step onto church ground or into space used by a church community is a side benefit, and a good one given our desire to serve and connect with people all around us." Rick Richardson, *You Found Me: New Research on How Unchurched Nones, Millennials, and Irreligious Are Surprisingly Open to Christian Faith* (Downers Grove, IL: IVP Books, 2019), 68-69.

can speak in a way that is accurate and understandable. For Christians, the ultimate revelation is in the person of Jesus of Nazareth, who presented us with the fullness of deity as a human being. Those of us who live after Jesus' earthly ministry trust the church's authorized accounts of his life as recorded in the Bible to give us an accurate depiction of him.

This appeal to revelation works when we interact with other people who share our belief in the legitimacy of the same sources of revelation. However, when we share our faith with people who do not agree about the truthfulness of the Bible or the authority of the church to determine the scriptural canon, our faith will be suspect to them. This is exactly the kind of epistemological resistance we have seen in the West as secularism has taken hold.

Combined with this, the church also has the problem of simple understandability. Groups of people often have language that is specific to them. Christians are no different. Whether this is in the form of technical vocabulary (e.g., atonement, sanctification) or metaphor (e.g., washed in the blood of the lamb, stars in our crowns) or stories (e.g., the parables of Jesus, the historical narratives of the people of Israel), a great deal of what Christians say and the ways we say it may not be recognizable or meaningful to the average person in a secular culture.

This is a problem that Christians have recognized for decades in the United States, with a variety of responses to it that have been adopted by congregations representing many of the theological traditions. One was to wipe away all uniquely Christian language and symbols from outward-facing church activities. The desired result of this was to remove any barrier between Christians and the people they sought to evangelize. The "Seeker Church" movement is the prime example of this. If people are comfortable enough in this more generic setting, they might decide to join the congregation and then can be brought into the faith more fully. The downside to this is that such a congregation may not be strong in developing people's faith because it has jettisoned so much to make people feel comfortable in the first place.

Another response has been to double down on unique Christian language. The reasoning behind this is that Christian language provides insights and concepts that are essential for people to understand, and these concepts are not available without using words that are distinctively Christian. By using this language, Christians will demonstrate that they have the framework to help people face the dangers of life and death. To prepare Christians to share their faith this way, congregations need to catechize their members so this language is first understandable and meaningful to them. The downside of this is that it can make the Christians sound irrelevant because they do not express themselves with language that is accessible to those outside the church. Worse, the catechized Christians might establish purity tests for who understands and believes rightly, rejecting those who have questions or doubts.

The experience of salvation as abundant life expressed in terms of standard of living, quality of life, and eternal life offers an approach that combines the best of both tactics while avoiding their pitfalls. By using language that is drawn from the secular world, it is understandable and meaningful for people outside the church. At the same time, because these terms are steeped in a biblical and theological commitment to proclaiming salvation as provided by God through Jesus Christ, they maintain the integrity of the Christian metanarrative.

This dual nature of the terms, as steeped in the logic of the Christian faith while being accessible to those outside the church, infuses the terms with new meaning for both Christians and those outside the church. The terms remind Christians that the abundant life of God continues unabated between this life and the next, and that abundant life must be participated in missionally rather than just received. The terms help those who are not Christian recognize, appreciate, and find meaning in how Christians participate in abundant life because they intersect with the common good. The terms also increase the credibility of the invitation Christians offer for others to know the salvation of Christ. As a result, these terms can enrich the theological traditions that use them by increasing their capacity to express their respective soteriologies to those outside the Christian faith.

Metrics. One meaningful way of expressing the Christian experience of salvation as abundant life in secular contexts is through quantifiable metrics. Particularly the terms *standard of living* and *quality of life* have metrics that have been developed and are used by many secular humanitarian aid organizations. This means that if Christians deploy these terms along with their metrics, they have a credible way of demonstrating the efficacy of Christian ministry to those outside of the Christian faith. They also can show in concrete ways how participating in abundant life includes working for the common good.

This addresses the critique that the Christian faith fails to have empirical evidence supporting its claims about the goodness God offers in this world. The metrics can offer this evidence in straightforward and compelling ways. For example, Christians can show that they have given a certain amount of money toward relieving the plight of those who are poor, housed a certain number of displaced refugees, and fed a certain number of malnourished children (indeed, Christian aid agencies already do publicize these sorts of numbers). These are all activities that work toward the common good and that show Christians are participating in abundant life by sharing the gifts they have received from God to save others from destructive forces in this world.

In addition to presenting the Christian message more persuasively in a secular culture, these metrics hold Christians accountable for living according to the salvation they claim. Jesus made it clear that those who follow him must share the gifts God has given them in ways that exceed how the secular world shares its gifts:

> If you love those who love you, what credit is that to you? For even sinners love those who love them. If you do good to those who do good to you, what credit is that to you? For even sinners do the same. If you lend to those from whom you hope to receive, what

credit is that to you? Even sinners lend to sinners, to receive as much again. But love your enemies, do good, and lend, expecting nothing in return. Your reward will be great, and you will be children of the Most High; for he is kind to the ungrateful and the wicked. (Luke 6:32-35 NRSV)

This is a hard teaching, which means it is easy for those of us who are Christians either to ignore it or to overestimate how well we are already obeying it. Using quantifiable measurements to record how much we work as individuals and communities to improve the standard of living and quality of life of others keeps us honest. It holds up a mirror that reflects the extent to which we just receive the abundant life of God and how much we participate in it by giving to others out of the resources God has made available to us.

This sort of measurement is not meant to determine who is saved eternally and who is not. It does, however, demonstrate how fully we have been formed in the character of Jesus, who "came not to be served but to serve, and to give his life a ransom for many" (Mark 10:45 NRSV). This avoids us looking like hypocrites to the secular culture by claiming to be disciples of Jesus but not following his example by seeking to alleviate the obvious suffering in the world.

Finally, the metrics would provide a means of welcome for those outside the Christian faith to work with and even within the church. This is not the same as claiming that those who are not Christians are anonymous Christians. If someone says they are not a Christian, then that person is not a Christian. However, not being a Christian does not preclude a person from sharing at least a portion of God's abundant life. With these metrics, we establish a bridge that allows us to communicate to people how we believe they are already responding to God's grace by how they are caring for others. We can prove this belief by working alongside them and by welcoming them to work alongside us. As we do so, we can share that the Christian gospel is the fulfillment of the work they are already doing, allowing them not just to improve standard of living and quality of life but to offer these as part of abundant life. This is much better than setting up the gospel in a way that just judges them.

This generous use for metrics is not an innovation. Rather, it follows the teaching of Jesus that we should encourage and not hinder those who seek to do good even if they are not a part of our community (Mark 9:38-41). We should look for whoever bears "good fruit" and acknowledge that God is active in that person's life (Luke 6:43-45). The Christian evangelist can then help these people learn more completely about what they are already doing.

These metrics let Christians demonstrate to those in the secular culture how wide the Christian faith is. They can see that we are not just trying to get them to become Christians but that we genuinely believe that God cares about all who suffer in this world. We could prove that this is not just rhetoric on our part because we would have the actions and hard numbers to back up our claim that we participate in abundant life by working to alleviate that suffering.

The wide scope of abundant life would enrich the traditions by requiring them not to limit their data collection only to the practices of the Christian faith they find most comfortable. They would need to expand their metrics to demonstrate that participating in abundant life orders every aspect of their adherents' lives and that they hold themselves accountable for this. In doing so, they would show that they cannot claim to live abundantly unless that abundance is visible in how they pour out the good gifts God has given them for the benefit of others in this world and the next.[26]

Exactly how these metrics would be collected and how they would measure participation in abundant life would be determined by each theological tradition. Each could shape its data collection to fit with its emphases. The appendix to this book offers some tools for how to do this.

---

[26]See the appendix for an example of how local congregations and individual Christians could gather these metrics.

Public discourse. The secularization of the West has gone hand in hand with the rise of pluralism. The increasing diversity of people and their belief systems has caused many Western cultures to embrace a nonsectarian, secular approach to avoid the appearance of giving preferential treatment to one set of people and their beliefs over another. In doing this, many individuals hope to appear neutral and open. The result of this in a pluralistic culture is to equate maintaining a secular stance with the common good.

Participating in abundant life entails working for the common good, but not in a way that accepts this secularist move. Instead, even as it motivates Christians to work alongside others, it offers a new vision for the common good. This vision honors the liberty accorded to people in pluralistic cultures without abandoning the Christian narrative. To make this vision clear requires Christians to engage in public discourse.

Miroslav Volf, a leading Christian scholar who studies how religion can operate in a pluralistic and secularized culture, together with Matthew Croasmun, developed guidelines for Christians to engage in public discourse in a way that neither capitulates to secularism nor demands that Christianity dominate all other beliefs. These guidelines are premised on a Christian understanding of a flourishing life.

Like the notion of abundant life from John 10:10, the flourishing life envisioned by Volf and Croasmun includes everything from basic human needs to culture, economics, politics, and a vision for the ultimate good. They explain, "Jesus did not just feed the poor and heal the sick, although he did that and stated explicitly that he came to do that; more importantly, he called them to reorient their entire lives around seeking God and God's righteousness."[27] To capture this fullness, they propose a tripartite structure for the flourishing life: "life going well, life led well, and life feeling as it should."[28] The first has to do with a person's standard of living, including the person's social, political, and economic location. The

---

[27]Miroslav Volf and Matthew Croasmun, *For the Life of the World* (Grand Rapids, MI: Brazos Press, 2019), 18.

[28]Volf and Croasmun, *For the Life of the World*, 16.

second has to do with the person's quality of life. How much do they enjoy the life they are leading? The third deals with how a person chooses to live. Do they live in a way that promotes good for themselves and for others? While this is not specifically a reference to eternal life, it points to the ethical mandate Jesus linked to being welcomed into eternal life (we will cover this in detail in chapter six).

Drawing together these three aspects of a flourishing life with the teachings of Paul, they suggest a Christian vision for a flourishing life is one that is at peace, that is filled with joy, and that is marked by righteous adherence to the covenant with God.[29] The whole of this flourishing life is a gift of the Holy Spirit.

Having received this gift, Christians are prepared to share their peace, joy, and righteousness in public discourse. The six guidelines Volf and Croasmun developed, grounded in the Christian narrative, offer directions for how to do this:

1. God sent Jesus for the good of all people, so Christians should seek to mend the world in every aspect of life.[30]

2. Christ's ministry was marked by grace, so Christians should not be coercive in their relationship with people in the larger culture.[31]

3. "A vision of human flourishing and the common good is the main thing the Christian faith brings into the public debate."[32]

4. "The proper stance of Christians toward the larger culture [is] . . . that of accepting, rejecting, learning from, transforming, and subverting or putting to better uses various elements of an internally differentiated and rapidly changing culture."[33]

5. "The way Christians work toward human flourishing is not by imposing on others their vision of human flourishing and the

---

[29]Volf and Croasmun, *For the Life of the World*, chap. 6.
[30]Volf and Croasmun, *For the Life of the World*, xv.
[31]Volf and Croasmun, *For the Life of the World*, xv.
[32]Volf and Croasmun, *For the Life of the World*, xvi.
[33]Volf and Croasmun, *For the Life of the World*, xvi.

common good but by bearing witness to Christ, who embodies the good life."[34]

6. "Christians, even those who in their own religious views are exclusivists, ought to embrace pluralism as a political project."[35]

At the heart of these guidelines is the belief that God works through Christ for the good of the entire world. There are no exceptions to this, regardless of what people believe or how they live. This provides the theological foundation for Christians to see goodness in a pluralistic culture rather than seeing it as a competitor for people's hearts and minds. At the same time, Christians can accept the benefits of cultural and political pluralism without acquiescing to secularism. As Volf explains, these guidelines provide "an alternative to totalitarian saturation of public life with a single religion as well as to secular exclusion of all religions from public life."[36]

Using these ground rules and guided by their vision of a flourishing life, Christians should engage with others graciously. This picks up on the same themes as participating in abundant life. As those who have accepted the abundant life that God offers through Christ, Christians are motivated to share that life fully with others. Volf reminds us that we do this not only through occasional acts of kindness toward those in need but with ongoing dialogue and gracious actions in the public square that offer an example of how Jesus treated others as we share our experience of God's salvation by participating in abundant life.

Many theological traditions were constructed out of intrareligious dialogue among Christians, not from dialogue with the larger culture (with the notable exception of many of the Majority World theologies). The opportunity to claim and adapt these guidelines for public discourse as a means of engaging with the larger culture enriches these traditions. It provides them a bridge to bring the wealth of how they express the gospel in a

---

[34]Volf, *A Public Faith* (Grand Rapids, MI: Brazos Press, 2011), xvi.
[35]Volf, *Public Faith*, xvii.
[36]Volf, *Public Faith*, xiv.

secular culture. It also provides them with a way of operating in a pluralistic context so they neither feel threatened by it nor assume the need to dominate it. Instead, they can overflow into it, motivated by the abundance of the life they have received and the desire to share that with others.

A BROADER VISION

Those who denied the resurrection sought to use the commonly known experience of bodies decomposing after death as a means of upending Paul's faith. Paul saw their trickery and answered their question by explaining that their experience was not large enough. Mortality and a decayed body were not the final experience for humans. Christians knew that a further experience was yet to take place: one in which the body was made imperishable and could live in its resurrected form forever. More than that, they knew that people did not need to wait until physical death to experience God's blessings. Through his life, death, and resurrection, Jesus had reshaped creation itself, making abundant life available for all who follow him now. That life would begin flowing in this world and would continue into eternity. This abundance was so thorough that it even sustained in the midst of suffering.

While their questions may not be the exact same as the one Paul faced, many people today would still consider the Christian faith out of step with common life experiences. Worse yet, their experiences of the Christian faith may have convinced them that Christians are hypocrites, failing to practice what they claim to believe, especially in terms of loving people the way Jesus loved them.

Too often, we as Christians miss this critique. Instead of answering it directly as Paul did, we pour our energy into debating over which theological tradition gets cultural precedence. What we fail to realize is that few people care. Whoever comes out on top is irrelevant because the vision of human experience that we are casting is still too small.

This is not just the experience of those outside the Christian faith. Within the global church, Christians from parts of the world with fewer resources find that their experiences of salvation are shut out from theological traditions. As a result, the salvation sought after and experienced by the Majority World is rarely reflected in formal soteriologies.

All this occurs because we tend to create Christian echo chambers, with those who adhere to specific theological traditions preferring to speak to one another. This avoids needing to learn new language for expressing our faith, having our beliefs held accountable by a review of our actions, and having to reflect on the assumptions undergirding our beliefs. To overcome this is not easy work. Many theological traditions have persisted for centuries and are averse to change.

The idea that Christians experience salvation through participating in abundant life, especially as explicated through the terms *standard of living*, *quality of life*, and *eternal life*, offers a leverage point to undertake that change by providing a broader vision for theological reflection than many traditions have used in the past. It requires those of us who hold to these traditions to contend with new words and constituencies that we may not have considered. This broader view is not meant to deconstruct but to enrich us with greater capacities to dialogue within the church and with the secular culture.

Expressing the Christian experience of salvation as participating in abundant life opens the doors for Christians from across geographical and theological traditions and for people in the secular culture alike to recognize the wideness of God's redemptive purposes. It undergirds and motivates Christians to be more active in the mission of God, deepening our faith and providing us with tangible and meaningful demonstrations of the Christian witness that those outside the Christian faith can recognize and appreciate.[37] It also offers a conceptual framework for

---

[37]While this is not primarily about church growth, it is notable that several studies by LifeWay Research point to the Christian witness being most effective at attracting new people to congregations when it entails improving standard of living and quality of life, as well as when it demonstrates greater racial and ethnic diversity in leadership. Aaron Earls, "7 Ways to Draw the Unchurched to Your Church," Lifeway Research, August 23, 2021, https://lifewayresearch.com /2021/08/23/7-ways-to-draw-the-unchurched-to-your-church/.

us to better understand each other throughout the world, drawing the global church closer together and normalizing the Majority World Christian experience.

Above all, it welcomes all people to receive life from God, "who by the power at work within us is able to accomplish abundantly far more than all we can ask or imagine" (Ephesians 3:20 NRSV). It does this by reminding us that as those who live in a universe that has been transformed by the life, death, and resurrection of Jesus Christ, abundance is the order in which we all operate now and into eternity by both receiving and giving. As Hirsch and Nelson ask when challenging the reduced imagination of the church related to salvation, "Why would we settle for a one-dimensional gospel when there is so much more good news to experience?"[38]

---

[38]Hirsch and Nelson, *Reframation*, 151.

3

Saving Lives

"SIRS, WHAT MUST I DO TO BE SAVED?"

This question is found on the lips of the jailer in Philippi who escaped a near-death experience thanks to the gracious work of the evangelists Paul and Silas. Overcome by their consideration for his life, he recognizes that the message they proclaimed must have merit and humbly asks them how to share in that salvation.

The jailer is not the only one in the Bible to ask a question like this. The rich young man asks Jesus, "What must I do to inherit eternal life" (Mark 10:17; Luke 18:18 NRSV)? A teacher of the law asked Jesus the same question (Luke 10:25). The large crowd that was "cut to the heart" when they listened to Peter on the day of Pentecost asked the apostles, "Brothers, what shall we do" (Acts 2:37)? Even as Isaiah lamented over how Israel's wickedness had cut them off from God's intervention, he asked on behalf of the nation, "How then can we be saved?" (Isaiah 64:5).

While the questions are similar, the motivations for asking are different in each situation. Some are concerned for their eternal destiny, some for their immediate well-being. The jailer's motivation included both. His life was in danger because he thought the prisoners had escaped during an earthquake, and Roman law required the death of the jailer in exchange for a lost prisoner. When Paul and Silas assured him that the prisoners had all remained, it was enough to bring the jailer to his knees. These men had sacrificed their freedom to save his life. What else might they teach him about being saved? Put in our parlance, they had already protected his standard of living and quality of life. Would they teach him how to participate in abundant life too? Paul and Silas readily agreed, going to his home, where they explained about the eternal life offered through Jesus Christ. There, the jailer and his family received the full salvation of Christ, a life saved in this world and in the next, and became participants in the abundant life of Christ by sharing their gifts with Paul and Silas through washing and dressing their wounds.

This passage and the other inquiries about salvation demonstrate that people who desire to be saved are looking for at least two things: (1) rescue from a danger they cannot overcome on their own and (2) assurance of a good life after that rescue. They are looking for abundant life.

A review of the full biblical witness, including the Hebrew Scriptures and the New Testament, shows that God recognizes the multiple ways people face harm in this world and the next and is ready to rescue them from all these dangers. God does this through improving their standard of living and quality of life as well as promising eternal life. God also invites those who are so blessed to participate in abundant life by sharing in God's life-giving work. This gives dignity to those who suffer by granting them agency to join God in improving their situations, and it offers a template for how people can share in the kingdom of God on earth. All of it offers insight to Christians on how they can provide a better witness to the abundant life available through Christ.

SALVATION IN THE HEBREW SCRIPTURES

The Hebrew Scriptures are not where Christians usually turn to reflect on salvation because we often see the visions of salvation in the Hebrew Scriptures as incomplete apart from Jesus. However, if we are to participate in abundant life, we need to take the teachings about salvation throughout the whole Bible seriously.

The Hebrew Scriptures focus more on how people operate in their daily lives than on how they prepare for eternity. This means that the views of salvation within the Hebrew Scriptures tend to deal with God's help for those in immediate and physical danger. As Walter Brueggemann explained in a conference on heaven,

> I am bound to say that this textual tradition has almost no interest in "heaven" as a place of hope in our usual sense, almost no specu- lation beyond the present space-time ordering of things. Indeed, "heaven" appears nowhere in the text as a place of appeal for "life after death," nowhere as a place where the dead go. . . . It is a hope rooted in heaven, not about *going there*, but about heaven—God's wondrous rule—*coming here* on earth.[1]

He further explained in the same presentation that "hope as a theological act cannot be extracted from this embedded, shaped, placed, lived reality."[2]

Far from this truncating the Christian witness, the emphasis in the Hebrew Scriptures on how God provides abundant life in the midst of "lived reality" enhances our ability to share our faith. It does this by al- lowing us to be more contextually meaningful, calling out the chaotic and evil forces that we see afflicting people in the world, explaining the ways that God saves people from suffering, and inviting those who are being harmed to take agency in bringing about their own rescue.

The suffering of chaos. A common plot in ancient Near Eastern mythology is that of a divine warrior overcoming the forces of chaos, with chaos often portrayed as the seas or a sea monster. The scholarly term given to this genre of literature is *Chaoskampf*. The Babylonians depicted their high god Marduk doing battle with the dragon Tiamat, who represented the chaotic saltwater of the sea. Only after Marduk's victory could he establish an orderly way of life that included agriculture and construction. Likewise, the Egyptians told the story of two of their eldest gods, Shu and Tefnut, who brought order to the primordial waters which were so powerful that the two gods nearly were lost within them.

---

[1]Walter Brueggemann, "The Hope of Heaven . . . on Earth," *Biblical Theology Bulletin* 29, no. 3 (August 1, 1999): 99-100.
[2]Brueggemann, "Hope of Heaven," 108.

There is extensive debate over the extent to which the creation story in Genesis picks up on the *Chaoskampf* genre since it depicts God speaking creation into existence with no hint of the primordial waters resisting or even having the agency to resist.[3] Moreover, the ongoing presence of the sea after creation suggests chaos is not fully destroyed by God. However, Old Testament scholar Bruce Birch comforts us with the idea that God intended this because God planned to live alongside humanity, providing protection and life for everyone throughout history: "Since chaos is not removed but controlled, God's activity in restraining chaos and sustaining order is a dimension in every generation."[4] Given this, salvation in the Hebrew Scriptures can be understood as occurring when God intervenes to help people out of the chaotic troubles they experience in this world.

According to the authors of the Hebrew Scriptures, these interpositions of chaos come through a variety of sources, including enemy armies, famines, plagues, the betrayal of friends, and evil spirits. However, the primary vehicle through which chaos emerges is the misuse of human agency called sin. According to Birch, "the implied moral norm is a measuring of human actions by reference to their faithfulness in reflecting God's will and ultimate rule."[5] When humans use their free will to act against God's will, they open the door for chaos and death in their lives as well as in all of creation. "In the Hebrew biblical tradition sin is treated as something that disturbs the whole of God's created order and not just the relationship between God and humanity."[6]

The idea that chaos is loose in the world, whether because of human sin or because of actions outside of human control, and that this chaos leads to massive devastation is something that resonates all too well today.

---

[3]See the helpful brief overview of authors who take differing positions on this in Charles Trimm, "Recent Research on War in the Old Testament," *Currents in Biblical Research* 10, no. 2 (March 12, 2012): 186.
[4]Bruce C. Birch, *Let Justice Roll Down: The Old Testament, Ethics, and Christian Life* (Louisville, KY: Westminster John Knox Press, 1991), 76.
[5]Birch, *Let Justice Roll Down*, 89.
[6]Birch, *Let Justice Roll Down*, 95.

A glance at today's headlines will verify this. As I write this, for example, the largest wildfire in California's history is scorching an area larger than the city of Los Angeles; the people of Yemen are starving to death after suffering under a brutal proxy war for years; hundreds are dead after several massive earthquakes have hit the Indonesian island of Lombok; and the Ebola virus has reemerged in the Democratic Republic of Congo. Two years later as I am revising this, we are living through the Covid-19 pandemic and the social turmoil brought about from years of institutional racism in the United States. The news when you are reading this will be different, but the persistence of chaos will still be there.

The Hebrew Scriptures affirm that God is not content to leave humanity wallowing in the chaotic consequences of its sin. To rescue humanity from this, God embarked on a process of redemption that is sometimes referred to as "salvation history," through which God would save both humanity and the rest of creation from the forces of chaos and bring them into a blessed state.

An earthly salvation. Birch suggests the Hebrew Scriptures' view of what it is like to experience salvation can be found by looking at what God intended for creation at the beginning. He describes it as being in a state of benevolence, relationality, and wholeness. Benevolence refers to both a physical and moral beauty in which everything lives in harmony and shares in the abundance of creation.[7] Relationality refers to humans living in interrelated community with each other as well as living interdependently with nature.[8] Wholeness, which Birch translates as the meaning of the Hebrew word *shalom*, "encompasses . . . justice, unity, well-being, joy, health, relationship, and peace."[9] Following the human move toward sin and chaos, God's work of salvation was to restore all of these traits to creation. It was to rescue people from death and restore them to the experience of abundant life.

---

[7]Birch, *Let Justice Roll Down*, 81.
[8]Birch, *Let Justice Roll Down*, 82.
[9]Birch, *Let Justice Roll Down*, 83.

The blessed state that Birch describes includes a high standard of living for everyone, both human and nonhuman, because all of creation would be renewed and abundant. It would offer a high quality of life because there would be nothing to fear or threaten us. It would look like the peaceable kingdom described in Isaiah 11:6-9:

> The wolf will live with the lamb,
>> the leopard will lie down with the goat,
> the calf and the lion and the yearling together;
>> and a little child will lead them.
> The cow will feed with the bear,
>> their young will lie down together,
>> and the lion will eat straw like the ox.
> The infant will play near the cobra's den,
>> and the young child will put its hand into the viper's nest.
> They will neither harm nor destroy
>> on all my holy mountain,
> for the earth will be filled with the knowledge of the LORD
>> as the waters cover the sea.

In this passage, the chaotic waters are limited to the sea, while the rest of creation resides safely on a mountain, far above the harmful reach of the waters. There, all creatures can rest contentedly while experiencing the excellent standard of living and quality of life that come from the benevolence, relationality, and wholeness of God's abundant life.

Such a vision is not just for those who believe in the biblical witness. It offers all people, regardless of their faith, a common source of inspiration and action. Everyone can have their hearts and minds enflamed with hope for a world in which all people's standard of living and quality of life are unsurpassed. This hope can even prompt people of goodwill toward generosity so that they are eager to share their resources with others in an effort to make this vision a reality.

As those who believe these words relate to an abundant life that over-flows to this world and the world to come, Christians should be at the forefront of sharing their resources. This would demonstrate that we un-derstand salvation must address the lived reality of helping people overcome the chaotic dangers in the world more than any words we could say. It would also show through our actions that we believe the abundant life we proclaim requires participation and sacrifice so others can share in it. This would provide proof that abundant life is not just a hope we pro-claim but the way we experience the presence of God's gracious work by allowing it to shape our character and inform how we use our resources.

Working for salvation in the Psalms. The Psalms add another facet to the experience of abundant life. Like the rest of the Hebrew Scriptures, they provide hope that God will move us past the chaos. However, they also acknowledge that exiting from chaos takes time and requires not only outside support but effort on the part of those who are suffering. As Walter Brueggemann puts it, "This hope is undeterred by circumstance, but is at the same time deeply candid about circumstance. The voice of Israel's faith makes clear beyond dispute that other powers still have a voice in our earthly governance, voices of death and disorder."[10]

In the Psalms, we encounter individuals who are searching for salvation as they suffer. Brueggemann provides a framework for this by categorizing each of the Psalms in terms of orientation, disorientation, and new orien-tation. Orientation psalms are those in which the authors describe a world that has not been disrupted. Everything is working well, and the authors are grateful for the status quo. Disorientation psalms are written by au-thors who have had their status quo shattered. These are often referred to as "complaint psalms" because of the brutally honest way the authors de-scribe their misery and demand for God to make things right. The new orientation psalms are penned by authors who offer God thanksgiving for carrying them through the pain of disorientation and bringing them to a

---

[10]Brueggemann, "Hope of Heaven," 100.

place of salvation. This salvation is not a return to the previous orientation but rather entails a new perspective about how the world works, born from the author's painful experiences of disorientation.[11]

Brueggemann developed this typology by adapting Paul Ricoeur's research on the use of language. Ricoeur studied how people used words based on both a text they were reading and the experiences they brought with them to that text. Based on his observations, Ricoeur concluded that people use words of hope and resistance in times of disorientation as well as words that let go of the past and embrace a new reality after they have passed through disorientation to a new orientation.[12] By adapting this research to his reading of the Psalms, Brueggemann appeals to words of faith and to a common human experience. He explains, "The Psalms bring human experience to sufficiently vivid expression so that it may be embraced as the real situations in which persons must live. This applies equally to the movement in the life of an individual person and to the public discernment of a new reality."[13] This emphasis on the lived reality expressed in the Psalms provides Christians with excellent examples of how individuals seek abundant life while they suffer.

The psalms of disorientation are most helpful in guiding the Christian witness when addressing people who are suffering. As Brueggemann explains it, these psalms have four parts:

1. Things are not right in the present arrangement.

2. They need not stay this way and can be changed.

3. The speaker will not accept the present arrangement, for it is intolerable.

4. It is God's obligation to change things.[14]

These psalms are uncensored in making their claims about the dangers and problems that their authors face. For example:

---

[11]Walter Brueggemann, *The Psalms and the Life of Faith*, ed. Patrick D. Miller (Minneapolis: Fortress Press, 1995), 24.

[12]Brueggemann, *Psalms and the Life of Faith*, 8-9.

[13]Brueggemann, *Psalms and the Life of Faith*, 27-28.

[14]Brueggemann, *Psalms and the Life of Faith*, 105.

LORD, how many are my foes!
How many rise up against me! (Psalm 3:1)

All night long I flood my bed with weeping
and drench my couch with tears.
My eyes grow weak with sorrow;
they fail because of all my foes. (Psalm 6:6-7)

My friends and companions avoid me because of my wounds;
my neighbors stay far away. (Psalm 38:11)

Even my close friend,
someone I trusted,
one who shared my bread,
has turned against me. (Psalm 41:9)

Whether it is being beset by enemies, experiencing betrayal by a close friend, dealing with illness, or facing depression, the psalms of disorientation share their authors' complaints unfiltered. "In every case, it is a circumstance in which the speaker lacks, in and of herself, resources to cope adequately with the crisis."[15] Put in the language we are using, disorientation psalms acknowledge that their authors' standard of living and quality of life are in peril, sometimes to the point of life-and-death struggles.

As severe as their situation is, though, Brueggemann suggests that the authors are not remaining passive as they cry out, doing nothing but waiting for divine intervention. They are also engaging in a practice of resistance by refusing to accept the situation. They assert that there is an alternative world of abundance and peace that can overthrow the current world of chaos and death.[16] Taking this stand is a means of asserting agency while enduring otherwise overwhelming suffering.

---

[15]Walter Brueggemann, *From Whom No Secrets Are Hid: Introducing the Psalms*, ed. Brent A. Strawn (Louisville, KY: Westminster John Knox, 2014), 87.

[16]For a much fuller description of this "counter world," see Brueggemann, *From Whom No Secrets Are Hid*, chap. 2.

When the problems encountered by the authors are caused by humans siding with the forces of chaos, this resistance opens the door for a political act of justice. "The cry mobilizes God in the arena of public life. . . . The response [is not a] simple religious succor, but it is the juridical action that rescues and judges. That is the nature of the function of the lament in Israel."[17]

Far from being a Marxist opiate of the masses that placates those who are hurting with the hope of an otherworldly salvation, the disorientation psalms rally the downtrodden and brokenhearted to the cause of justice. Without this call to action, the psalms lose their power. Brueggemann even goes so far as to say that when such psalms are silenced in the community of faith, people of faith begin to believe that

> justice questions are improper . . . in public places, in schools, in hospitals, with the government, and eventually even in the courts. Justice questions disappear into civility and docility. The order of the day comes to seem absolute, beyond question, and we are left with only grim obedience and eventual despair.[18]

If they are allowed to speak, though, the disorientation psalms can become the first glimmer of salvation by inviting those who suffer to participate in the restoration of their own lives. This is not a matter of salvation by self-help. Only God has the power of life to bring victory over the forces of chaos and death. However, God invites those who suffer to participate in the power of life so they can work to alleviate their suffering and perhaps even the suffering of others.

Christians should include this empowerment as part of our witness to those who suffer. As important as it is for us to share our resources to improve the standard of living and quality of life of others, we are not just to be the benefactors. This runs the risk of our falling into colonial and paternalistic practices. We should also stand in solidarity with those who suffer, strengthening their agency to work toward a better standard of

---

[17]Brueggemann, *Psalms and the Life of Faith*, 107.
[18]Brueggemann, *Psalms and the Life of Faith*, 107.

living and quality of life for themselves. Participating in abundant life includes joining those who suffer so we can amplify their cry for relief and justice.

Altogether, then, the Hebrew Scriptures inform our Christian witness by teaching us to:

1. Articulate the reality of the suffering that people face in this world as well as the hope we have for God's power to overcome that suffering in this world.

2. Recognize that all good gifts we have in this world come from God and are to be used to bless others.

3. Give the gifts we have received from God in this world to improve the standard of living and/or quality of life of those who suffer.

4. Advocate for justice on behalf of those whose diminished standard of living and quality of life are caused by human sin.

5. Join with those who suffer with our advocacy, recognizing that they have agency to work for justice to be established.

This guidance is biblical, practical, and meaningful to people outside the Christian faith. Even the famed atheist Christopher Hitchens could appreciate a view of salvation that works for justice on behalf of the those who have been wronged, as shown by his advocacy on behalf of those who were abused by Catholic clergy.[19] This is because the Hebrew Scriptures' description of how God's people can participate in abundant life in this world intersects with the universal human desire for salvation from the forces of chaos that harm people's standard of living and quality of life.

THE NEW TESTAMENT AND THE KINGDOM OF GOD

The salvation history begun in the Hebrew Scriptures continues in the New Testament. The New Testament is no less concerned than the

---

[19]Christopher Hitchens, "A Call for Earthly Justice," *Slate*, September 13, 2010, www.slate.com /articles/news_and_politics/fighting_words/2010/09/a_call_for_earthly_justice.html.

Hebrew Scriptures with God's abundant life rescuing people from the chaos and sin in the world through improved standard of living and quality of life. The new detail the New Testament brings to this story is that God makes that abundant life available both in this world and eternally through Jesus Christ. The New Testament describes the experience of participating in this abundant life through Christ as being part of the kingdom of God.

Jesus Christ inaugurated the kingdom of God by defeating the powers of chaos and sin through his life, death, and resurrection. While these powers still exist and can cause harm to people, people are nonetheless able to live as subjects of the kingdom by accepting the victory of Christ. Jesus promised to return in the future and establish the kingdom of God in its fullness, sweeping away chaos, sin, and even death eternally. In the interim between the inauguration and final consummation of the kingdom, Jesus calls people to participate in abundant life as his disciples. Those who become his disciples join in Jesus' mission to share abundant life with all people by working to improve others' standard of living and quality of life as well as by teaching them the gospel of eternal life. All of this is done not just to bless others but as a means of inviting them to likewise become disciples of Jesus who participate in abundant life.

Jesus, abundant life, and the kingdom of God. Jesus taught that to become his disciple and enter the kingdom of God, people must repent, turning away from activities that promote chaos and sin in the world toward righteousness and life. This repentance would lead to a trans-formed way of life, with new ethics guiding how people relate to one another and make moral decisions. Jesus promised that God would provide for those who made this shift to enter the kingdom:

> So do not worry, saying, "What shall we eat?" or "What shall we drink?" or "What shall we wear?" For the pagans run after all these things, and your heavenly Father knows that you need them. But seek first his kingdom and his righteousness, and all these things will be given to you as well. (Matthew 6:31-33)

Of particular importance in this passage are the examples that Jesus uses. He is not talking about spiritual blessings that people will receive in some distant future. He is talking about the kingdom of God being present in tangible ways for those who seek it. They would have clothes to wear, food to eat, and beverages to drink. In other words, the abundant life of the kingdom begins here and now by providing for people's standard of living and quality of life.

Jesus supported this teaching with compassionate acts that demonstrated God's power to improve people's lives in this world. He fed people when they were hungry, healed people afflicted with a wide range of illnesses, cast out demons from those overcome by evil powers, restored people who had been cut off from community, and raised the dead to life. In doing this, he made it clear that he was not just pointing to a future time when the kingdom of God would arrive but declaring that the abundant life of the kingdom was available now. As he explained to those who questioned the authority he had to drive out demons, "If I drive out demons by the finger of God, then the kingdom of God has come upon you" (Luke 11:20). He made the same point when he was asked what events would inaugurate the kingdom of God. He replied that the kingdom was already present in his ministry:

> Once Jesus was asked by the Pharisees when the kingdom of God was coming, and he answered, "The kingdom of God is not coming with things that can be observed; nor will they say, 'Look, here it is!' or 'There it is!' For, in fact, the kingdom of God is among you." (Luke 17:20-21 NRSV)

The improved standard of living and quality of life Jesus provided was a manifestation of the abundant life of God's reign in the face of the ongoing chaos people endured. However, Jesus provided more than just a sign of the kingdom's presence through the immediate alleviation of people's suffering. He overcame the destructive forces of chaos, sin, and death completely.

For the New Testament authors, the resurrection of Jesus, especially after his horrific torture and crucifixion, reframed reality. The forces of sin and chaos were overthrown. Death itself was undone. The worst that the world and the powers of darkness could do had been marshaled against Jesus, and he had emerged victorious.

In making these claims, the New Testament authors echoed how the Hebrew Scriptures described God overcoming chaos. The Gospels depict chaos and darkness shrouding the betrayal and crucifixion of Jesus giving way to the light of the resurrection early in the morning. Later, the book of Revelation draws on the images of overcoming chaos to describe the final coming of the kingdom.[20] Prior to the kingdom's establishment, it declares that the primordial waters of chaos are no longer a danger, stating that the sea is so calm in the presence of God that it is like glass (Revelation 4:6; 15:2). Once God's reign is fully consummated, the sea is entirely absent (21:1). In its place is a renewed heaven and earth where there is "no more death or mourning or crying or pain" (21:4) and where a river of life waters trees that provide "for the healing of the nations" (22:2 NRSV).

This is the conclusion of the ancient *Chaoskampf,* with chaos nowhere to be found and abundant life flowing unhindered and eternally. This is the final, glorious experience of abundant life. Christians should find strength and hope in this, allowing them to be a perpetual beacon of hope. No matter how dreary or chaotic the world becomes, we believe the kingdom of God will be fulfilled in the end. We know this because Jesus died and rose again. Nothing is left that can stand in the way of God's life. More than this, we believe that we can operate out of the kingdom even now, trusting God to provide for our needs as we serve in God's mission.

A life for mission. The New Testament records Jesus commissioning his disciples to carry out his mission of making more disciples in five passages. Again, this is not just a matter of calling people to a spiritual commitment but of sharing God's abundant life. In each of the five passages, Jesus instructs his disciples to offer life in multiple ways (see figure 3.1).

---

[20]Dominic Rudman, "The Crucifixion as Chaoskampf: A New Reading of the Passion Narrative in the Synoptic Gospels," *Biblica* 84 (2003): 102-7.

And Jesus came and said to them, "All authority in heaven and on earth has been given to me. Go therefore and make disciples of all nations, baptizing them in the name of the Father and of the Son and of the Holy Spirit, and teaching them to obey everything that I have commanded you. And remember, I am with you always, to the end of the age." (Matthew 28:18-20 NRSV)	Jesus commissions the disciples to participate in abundant life by improving others' quality of life through welcoming them into the community of believers. Jesus will personally be with the disciples, providing for them as they carry out this work.
And he said to them, "Go into all the world and proclaim the good news to the whole creation. The one who believes and is baptized will be saved; but the one who does not believe will be condemned. And these signs will accompany those who believe: by using my name they will cast out demons; they will speak in new tongues; they will pick up snakes in their hands, and if they drink any deadly thing, it will not hurt them; they will lay their hands on the sick, and they will recover." (Mark 16:15-18 NRSV)	Jesus promises his disciples will have access to supernatural means of sharing God's abundant life, including improving people's standard of living by healing them, improving their quality of life by overcoming oppressive evil forces, and assuring them of eternal life if they believe on Jesus Christ.
He said to them, "Thus it is written, that the Messiah is to suffer and to rise from the dead on the third day, and that repentance and forgiveness of sins is to be proclaimed in his name to all nations, beginning from Jerusalem. You are witnesses of these things. And see, I am sending upon you what my Father promised; so stay here in the city until you have been clothed with power from on high." (Luke 24:46-49 NRSV)	Jesus tells his disciples to welcome people into eternal life through the forgiveness of sins, made available through Jesus' resurrection. The disciples will have power to do this work through the Holy Spirit.
Jesus said to them again, "Peace be with you. As the Father has sent me, so I send you." When he had said this, he breathed on them and said to them, "Receive the Holy Spirit. If you forgive the sins of any, they are forgiven them; if you retain the sins of any, they are retained." (John 20:21-23 NRSV)	Jesus invites the disciples into a deeper experience of abundant life by breathing the Spirit into them, then commissions them to act in the power of the Spirit to forgive others.
He replied, "It is not for you to know the times or periods that the Father has set by his own authority. But you will receive power when the Holy Spirit has come upon you; and you will be my witnesses in Jerusalem, in all Judea and Samaria, and to the ends of the earth." (Acts 1:7-8 NRSV)	Jesus clarifies that the disciples are to move in the power of the Spirit to share the abundant life of God with everyone in the world. God's life will not diminish by being shared extensively.

Figure 3.1. Commissioned to share abundant life

Taken together, these passages show that those who undertake the mission of God to make disciples are participating in abundant life. They have been saved through receiving the abundant life of God through their faith in Jesus, and they are called to share that abundant life with others in the power of the Holy Spirit. They share it by inviting people to believe on Jesus so they can be forgiven of their sins and assured of eternal life as well as through improving people's standard of living and quality of life.

As the first disciples carried out this mission, the New Testament records that they were careful to follow the example of Jesus' humble life and death. Even though Jesus was God incarnate, he chose a life of service and sacrifice instead of conquest and glory. His quest was not for his own salvation but for the salvation of others. He persisted in this even when it caused him pain and suffering.

This is not to say that Christians believe they had to earn their way into God's salvation. Jesus did not neurotically seek to do good deeds to gain God's favor. Rather, it was out of the assurance that his life was already secured by God that Jesus could offer God's life to those around him (John 13:3-5). His example shows Christians that sharing the abundant life of God with others is the natural overflow of having received that abundant life (Matthew 10:8).

The disciples and early church sought to build on this example. They worked to improve people's standard of living through taking up collections to provide for the needs of the poor (1 Corinthians 16:1-4; 2 Corinthians 8) and distributing food to widows (Acts 6:1). They also improved people's quality of life through establishing ethical structures that promoted community formation and reconciliation by inviting the wealthy and poor into a common fellowship where favoritism toward the wealthy was expressly forbidden (James 2:1-4), welcoming Jews and Gentiles as equal recipients of God's grace who can look toward the consummation of the kingdom of God

(Acts 11:1-18), and valuing women for their gifts by giving them places in leadership (Philippians 4:2-3).[21]

This work sometimes involved Christians sacrificing on behalf of others. In these cases, the Christians would willingly lessen their standard of living to increase someone else's, such as by giving away large sums of money to support the needy. This did not mean they were participating in abundant life any less or that the amount of life they had available to them decreased. Rather, by following the example of Christ through sacrificing their standard of living for others, Christians would gain a higher quality of life because they had a greater sense of joy for participating in the work of God. Moreover, their standard of living would not drop because the community would care for them.

The generosity of the Macedonian Christians in giving to relieve the plight of others stands out as an example of this. According to Paul, these Christians gave a large amount even though they were poor:

> During a severe ordeal of affliction, their abundant joy and their extreme poverty have overflowed in a wealth of generosity on their part. For, as I can testify, they voluntarily gave according to their means, and even beyond their means, begging us earnestly for the privilege of sharing in this ministry to the saints. (2 Corinthians 8:2-4 NRSV)

While they decreased in standard of living because they had less money to secure goods and services for themselves, they increased in quality of life because of the joy they experienced from giving to help others. They experienced God's abundant life more fully by giving than by just receiving.

This takes the idea from the psalms about God empowering those who suffer to work for their own betterment to the next level. Here, those who

---

[21]It is worth noting that, while carried out by Christians to demonstrate the alternative ethics of God's reign, these are all activities that fit with the UN Sustainable Development Goals today. The UN Sustainable Development Goals are the internationally agreed-on guides for creating a new world order that improves standard of living and quality of life for people around the globe. We will explore them in greater detail in chapter 6. For reference, in this example, Goal 1 is to end poverty, Goal 5 is to achieve gender equality, and Goal 16 is to promote peaceful and inclusive societies.

suffer also have agency to bless others. Even those who are poor can give financially to help those in need. God's abundant life overflows to give everyone agency to participate in God's mission by sharing with others.

This increased joy comes not only through sacrificing for others but as a result of suffering for the sake of Christ. Jesus taught in the Beatitudes, "Blessed are you when people revile you and persecute you and utter all kinds of evil against you falsely on my account. Rejoice and be glad, for your reward is great in heaven, for in the same way they persecuted the prophets who were before you" (Matthew 5:11-12 NRSV). The apostles took this teaching to heart, as seen in one of the earliest moments of persecution they endured. After being flogged for preaching about Jesus publicly, "they rejoiced that they were considered worthy to suffer dishonor for the sake of the name [of Jesus]" (Acts 5:41 NRSV). Historian Darin McMahon reflected on this Christian ability to experience joy in suffering:

> Christianity . . . propos[ed] that happiness was not just impervious to pain, but its direct outcome and consequence. The rack, the instrument of torture—the cross—becomes the site and symbol of a more general process of conversion, a place of spiritual alchemy where the base metal of human pain is converted into the gold of divine rapture. With good reason is Christ's suffering and death termed the "passion." His infinite capacity to experience anguish is directly proportionate to his infinite capacity to convey the experience of joy.[22]

The New Testament does not advocate for this sort of self-denial out of a moral disdain of fun, an inherent rejection of wealth and "the good life," or a morbid belief that God wants us to be in pain, but out of a desire for all people to enter the kingdom of God and experience abundant life. Jesus explained in the Sermon on the Mount that those who seek the kingdom before all else will have everything provided for them. He made

---

[22]Darrin M. McMahon, *Happiness: A History* (New York: Grove Press, 2006), 95.

this point even more explicitly in the Gospel of Mark, promising good things in the present world and the assurance of eternal life for those who were faithful to the mission:

> Jesus said, "Truly I tell you, there is no one who has left house or brothers or sisters or mother or father or children or fields, for my sake and for the sake of the good news, who will not receive a hundredfold now in this age—houses, brothers and sisters, mothers and children, and fields, with persecutions—and in the age to come eternal life." (Mark 10:29-30 NRSV)

To participate in abundant life is to claim this promise even if it requires suffering for the sake of being faithful in Jesus' mission.

The Story of Salvation

The Bible is the story of salvation. It tells of God rescuing people who are overwhelmed by the chaotic waters and lifting them to a paradise where chaos itself is no more. The chaos seeks our death and the death of creation. God's salvation offers life so abundant that death is swept away and creation is renewed. This life overcomes death in many ways throughout the biblical literature, meeting the specific needs of those who must be rescued: it can be protection from enemies, joy to replace despair, provisions in a time of scarcity, healing when facing sickness, community for the lonely, or even the dead being raised to life. In short, the Bible affirms that God's salvific work includes improving people's standard of living and quality of life in addition to providing them eternal life.

The kingdom of God, inaugurated through the life, death, and resurrection of Jesus Christ, is the fulfillment of this salvific work. In the kingdom, we receive the abundant life of God unhindered forever. However, the kingdom has not yet fully come. As we wait for its eschatological consummation, Christians are called not just to receive the abundant life of God but to participate in it through sharing God's abundant life with others.

The question is not whether Christians can claim that serving as witnesses to God's abundant life through Christ, including through improving people's standard of living and quality of life as well as preaching the gospel of eternal life, is an activity that can be done with integrity related to the biblical witness. It assuredly is. The question, rather, is how Christians can bring their unique message of the gospel to bear in working for these improvements for others. This is what we will consider in the next two chapters.

As we consider this, it is important to remember that the biblical story of salvation does not disallow Christians from making common cause with people of goodwill regardless of their faith commitments. Christians across the theological spectrum can agree on doing good to all people, following the holistic example of God's salvific work in Christ. Even those who hold to other faiths or no faith can recognize and appreciate the desire to work for the common good, especially on behalf of those in the greatest need in this world. The missional call of Christians should not hinder this work. Rather, it should spur this work on while prompting Christians to witness to those they are working alongside by demonstrating their ability to find joy even when they must sacrifice or suffer for the name of Christ.

4

Standard of Living

*Defend the weak and the fatherless; uphold the cause
of the poor and the oppressed. Rescue the weak and
the needy; deliver them from the hand of the wicked.*

PSALM 82:3-4

WE ALL HAVE SEEN THE COMMERCIALS. Impoverished children
stare at the camera. With their rib bones and stomachs protruding, it is
easy to see that they are desperately malnourished and hungry. The
camera pans over their grimacing faces. The scene shifts to the inside of
a makeshift hospital where anxious parents hold tiny babies crying for
food and attention. The narrator lets us know that there are thousands
more like these.

In an attempt to escape, we change the channel or turn off the television and take out our phones. Our efforts are in vain, though. The news
we encounter is full of images of people who have been overwhelmed by
the latest disasters, both natural and manmade. Houses sit underwater,
inundated by the torrential rains from the latest hurricane or shredded
by tornadoes; apartment complexes are toppled by earthquakes; and
refugees flee into overcrowded camps as bombs rain down on the neighborhoods where they once lived.

It is not surprising that humanitarian aid organizations of all types
present us with these sorts of pictures and stories when requesting

donations or that news outlets will include links to agencies where we can give to help those affected by the disasters they report. All these scenes tug at our heartstrings regardless of our faith. These are human problems. They demonstrate a kind of privation we can feel on a visceral level and spark our deepest fears. But for the grace of God, we could be in the same situation, struggling to survive without the basic implements to care for our, or our children's, needs.

All these scenes deal with standard of living. Standard of living is measured by tracking a person's income and consumption. Income indicates the amount of resources that a person or household has available to procure goods and services from the market. Consumption, which can occur by purchasing goods and services or through household production (e.g., growing one's own vegetables), measures the extent to which a person or household can access and make use of those goods and services.[1] The lower a person's standard of living, the fewer goods and services that person can access and use. In extreme cases, a person has difficulty accessing the necessities of life, such as food, water, housing, and medical care. A wealthy person who is forced to abandon her house because of floodwaters cannot access shelter in the way she once did even though she has a high income. A person living below the poverty threshold may live where there are plentiful goods available for purchase but lack the income to buy them. Both suffer from a low standard of living in these scenarios (although the long-term impact of these situations is quite different).

While seeing people in such desperate straits can be uncomfortable for us, the one positive is that we can do something about it. People struggling with a low standard of living often face an immediate and acute crisis that can be alleviated. As long as those of us who have a high

---

[1]Owen O'Donnell, Eddy van Doorslaer, Adam Wagstaff, and Magnus Lindelow, *Analyzing Health Equity Using Household Survey Data: A Guide to Techniques and Their Implementation* (Washington, DC: World Bank, 2008), 69. There is a substantial literature that delves into the various methodologies and complexities of measuring standard of living. For the sake of this book, we will remain at this basic level of definition.

standard of living are willing to share with those who have a low standard of living, we can usually meet their needs. If someone does not have enough food, we can buy food for that person and ship it to them. If someone lacks medical attention, we can send doctors to tend them. If someone lacks housing, we can build a house and move them into it.

Structural changes may have to occur beyond meeting these immediate needs to make certain that those we share with can maintain a higher standard of living. In the interim, though, we can at least get them over the hump of starvation, illness, homelessness, or whatever other lack of resources besets them. We often benefit from this by seeing our help make a difference in real time as the hungry eat, the sick are cared for, and the homeless are sheltered. Our quality of life goes up as we share.

It is in addressing these needs that the idea of salvation intersects with standard of living. In helping people who are suffering because of a low standard of living, we offer them a tangible form of Christ's abundant life. They experience salvation by receiving the physical means for life to rescue them from deprivation, pain, and, in the most extreme cases, death. We experience salvation by participating in abundant life through stewarding the provisions God has given us in a way that provides for others in need.

COMPONENTS OF STANDARD OF LIVING

Although at its most basic level standard of living addresses what humans need to survive, in most cases a person's standard of living is defined contextually. It is "the level of economic welfare and consumer satisfaction, strictly in terms of economic well-being, of a given economic context."[2] This means that standard of living focuses on how well-off people are economically in a specific region. A high standard of living in one country or region of the world will look different from another

---

[2]Luca A. Panzone, "Measuring Standards of Living," in *Encyclopedia of Consumer Culture*, ed. Dale Southerton (Thousand Oaks, CA: SAGE, 2011), 932.

country or region.[3] Put another way, it is different to be poor in Belgium than in Laos, Peru, or Hong Kong.

Large NGOs, such as the United Nations (UN), measure standard of living in a way that allows them to compare one country's economic well-being to another's. This sort of measurement looks at factors that come as a result of a higher standard of living for an entire population rather than the actual consumption of goods. The Human Development Index is an example of this, which measures life expectancy at birth, average years of schooling for children, the mean years of schooling for adults age twenty-five and above, and the gross national income per capita. All these items are premised on the availability of goods and services a population can consume and on the income the population has to purchase those things. The more food, medical care, and other necessities of life people can consume, the more likely they are to live longer and attain higher levels of education. The higher the per capita income, the more people will have stable access to maintaining that consumption. With this data, the UN seeks to determine the economic strength of each nation.

These large economic calculations do not show the variation of standard of living within nations, the reasons people face a low standard of living, or how long they have been in that situation. The desperate need seen in the wake of disasters is one example of how the sudden curtailment of income and/or ability to consume the necessities of life can affect the way people live, but this is often dealt with relatively swiftly. Within a year or so, victims of this lower standard of living are restored to their original way of life. However, a low standard of living can be a persistent problem. Poverty is the result of people having a low income coupled with the inability to consume goods and services over an extended period of time. The less income and/or consuming capacity a person has, the poorer that person is.

---

[3]This is an important point related to foreign mission work. Al Tizon, former president of the American Society of Missiology, explained this in his presidential address, later published as "Lifestyles of the Rich and Faithful: Confronting Classism in Christian Mission," *Missiology* 48, no. 1 (January 2020): 23.

The impact of poverty. The effects of poverty are wide-ranging. Because people living below the poverty threshold are incapable of consuming at a level that is considered normal for the region where they live, they are often excluded from a wide variety of economic and social relations. This is especially so in developed countries where economies are driven by consumer spending, making consumption at a certain level necessary for social interaction.[4] Consider, for example, the expectation that everyone has watched the latest streaming television show or obtained the latest phone or experienced how maddening it is for computers to update software suddenly in the middle of a project. These are common enough occurrences for those that can afford to consume all the goods and services mentioned. However, if your income is below the poverty threshold, you are left out of the social loop because you cannot consume these.

This exclusion extends beyond those who are poor not being able to afford to shop in certain stores or consume specific goods. It also manifests in the perspectives nonpoor people have of those who are poor. Consider the discomfort that many people have making eye contact with the homeless person (someone with such a low standard of living that they cannot consume basic shelter) they encounter when they walk down the street or drive up to an intersection. As one child from a poor neighborhood in England reported during a survey of youth and poverty in the United Kingdom, "The worst thing about living in poverty is the way it gives others permission to treat you as if you don't matter."[5]

The economic and social implications of a person's standard of living are so strong that there is a measurable impact on the emotional well-being of those who face a sudden drop in their personal standard of living. In a study of the population of Iceland, which suffered a serious economic shock during the 2008 economic downturn, researchers found

---

[4]Terhi-Anna Wilska, "State Provisioning," in Southerton, *Encyclopedia of Consumer Culture*, 1377.
[5]Barry Knight, *Rethinking Poverty: What Makes a Good Society?* (Bristol, England: Bristol University Press, 2017), 76.

that people who believed either that their standard of living had dropped further than their peers or that they would be less likely to improve their standard of living compared to their peers in the future had higher rates of feeling anger or a sense of injustice.[6] This was at least partly attributable to how their new standard of living made them feel less like a part of the society around them.

The UN Sustainable Development Goals witness to the wider effect of poverty. To help the world's most impoverished people, multiple steps must be taken to address all the aspects of life that are diminished by poverty or that contribute to disallowing people a reasonable income and/or ability to consume.

United Nations Sustainable Development Goals:

1. End poverty in all its forms everywhere

2. End hunger, achieve food security and improved nutrition, and promote sustainable agriculture

3. Ensure healthy lives and promote well-being for all at all ages

4. Ensure inclusive and equitable quality education and promote lifelong learning opportunities for all

5. Achieve gender equality and empower all women and girls

6. Ensure availability and sustainable management of water and sanitation for all

7. Ensure access to affordable, reliable, sustainable, and modern energy for all

8. Promote sustained, inclusive, and sustainable economic growth, full and productive employment, and decent work for all

9. Build resilient infrastructure, promote inclusive and sustainable industrialization, and foster innovation

10. Reduce inequality within and among countries

---

[6]Berglind Hólm Ragnarsdóttir, Jón Gunnar Bernburg, and Sigrún Ólafsdóttir, "The Global Financial Crisis and Individual Distress: The Role of Subjective Comparisons After the Collapse of the Icelandic Economy," *Sociology* 47, no. 4 (August 2013): 770.

11. Make cities and human settlements inclusive, safe, resilient, and sustainable

12. Ensure sustainable consumption and production patterns

13. Take urgent action to combat climate change and its impacts (taking note of agreements made by the UNFCCC forum)

14. Conserve and sustainably use the oceans, seas, and marine resources for sustainable development

15. Protect, restore, and promote sustainable use of terrestrial ecosystems, sustainably manage forests, combat desertification and halt and reverse land degradation, and halt biodiversity loss

16. Promote peaceful and inclusive societies for sustainable development, provide access to justice for all, and build effective, accountable, and inclusive institutions at all levels

17. Strengthen the means of implementation and revitalize the global partnership for sustainable development[7]

This is a clear cause-and-effect: if unchecked, a lower standard of living measured by a lack of income and/or ability to consume leads to poverty, which, in turn, leads to a variety of social, economic, and emotional problems. Fortunately, this domino effect can be halted. If we intervene at the initial point of loss by either boosting income or boosting access to the goods that people are otherwise unable to consume, then we may arrest the entire process. This is certainly the hope we have as we hold drives to collect food and other supplies for people afflicted by a sudden crisis. If we can provide the necessities of life quickly enough, they will still be able to consume on par with the rest of us and not fall outside the consumerist structure of society. The same logic is often used in seeking to alleviate longer-term poverty. If we can provide homes for the homeless, sustainable sources of food for the persistently hungry, durable clothing for

---

[7]"Sustainable Development Goals," United Nations, www.un.org/sustainabledevelopment /sustainable-development-goals/.

the naked, and ongoing treatment for the sick, we can lay the groundwork for people to exit poverty and enter more fully into social relations.

Humanitarian aid and Christian mission. This work to improve people's standard of living is usually termed *humanitarian aid* and is something that nearly all people, regardless of their faith or lack thereof, can agree on as a necessary activity for the common good. Religious leaders are seen as important partners in this work. One example of this is the Alliance of Religions and Conservation (ARC), an organization launched in England in 1995 that brings together leaders from a variety of religions to work with the United Nations in implementing the Sustainable Development Goals. In 2015 when the goals were being introduced, then Secretary General of the UN Ban Ki-moon wrote to the ARC explaining the importance of religion in humanitarian work:

> Faith leaders are well placed to build bridges of understanding and cooperation. They provide vital relief, health and education to their communities, and ensure the inclusion of otherwise excluded and neglected groups and communities. Such contributions are especially important at [a] time when strong global leadership is required to solve escalating humanitarian challenges.[8]

Responding to this call for leadership in supporting the new goals, twenty-three faith communities, including those holding to the Baha'i, Buddhist, Daoist, Hindu, Islamic, Jewish, Shinto, and Sikh faiths, as well as several Christian communions, presented plans for how they would support this humanitarian work in their contexts. These included ways to measure their effectiveness in improving people's standard of living.

While not a part of the ARC, the Catholic Church also embraced the Sustainable Development Goals. Connecting these goals to the papal encyclical *Laudato Si'*, the *Laudato Si'* Covenant was formed to address

---

[8]Alliance of Religions and Conservation, *Faith in the Future: Bristol Commitments* (Bath, UK: Alliance of Religions and Conservation in association with the United Nations Development Program, 2015), 7.

the goals related to climate change and poverty in concrete ways. This includes planting one billion bamboo propagules and developing sustainable local bamboo industries, creating accessible digital education for one million out-of-school youth, and networking one million organic farmers through an e-commerce platform. In developing this, "Pope Francis called not only on Catholics but on all people of goodwill, no matter what the race, creed, or nationality to take up the sustainability challenge."[9]

Secular and religious agreement over the need to improve people's standard of living is especially visible when there is a major disaster. One such example is the plight of the Rohingya people in Bangladesh and Myanmar during the late 2010s.

With approximately one million people living in refugee camps or makeshift villages, the Rohingya have been forced to endure extreme poverty, poor health conditions, sex trafficking, and violence. Their dire need has attracted the attention of several major humanitarian agencies from around the world, including Médecins Sans Frontières (MSF), known in English as Doctors Without Borders, and Catholic Relief Services (CRS).

MSF has made caring for the Rohingya one of its chief activities. They report:

> MSF teams carried out more than 656,200 medical consultations and treated 13,179 inpatients between August 2017 and June 2018. The most common conditions treated were respiratory infections, diarrheal diseases, and skin diseases—all related to poor living conditions. Teams have also worked to improve water and sanitation services, constructing more sustainable latrines, drilling boreholes and tube wells, and installing a gravity-fed water supply system.[10]

---

[9]Fr. Benigno P. Beltran, SVD, "Earth Stewardship, Economic Justice, and World Mission: The Teachings of *Laudato Si'*," *Missiology* 48, no. 1 (January 2020): 43.

[10]"The Rohingya Refugee Crisis," Médecins Sans Frontières, accessed February 4, 2021, www .doctorswithoutborders.org/rohingya-refugee-crisis.

In addition to the diseases they treated and the sanitation they provided, MSF also conducted 17,671 mental health consultations. These were to help those who had experienced or witnessed extreme violence, especially children.

CRS also made working with the Rohingya a priority. As of November 2017, CRS had distributed a two-month supply of food and kitchen sets to 10,000 families (helping a total of approximately 68,000 people). Beyond this, they were working with local partners to establish permanent sources of food, shelter, water, sanitation, hygiene, and protection. They had already procured sufficient floormats and bedding to assist 10,200 households.[11]

Both organizations engaged in this work even though their motivation is quite different. MSF makes it clear that they are neutral in all ways. This includes being nonsectarian since they will not identify with any religious belief. The MSF Charter states,

Médecins Sans Frontières/Doctors Without Borders (MSF) is a private international association founded in 1971. The association is made up mainly of doctors and health sector workers and is also open to other professions which might help in achieving its aims. Our mission is to provide lifesaving medical care to those most in need.

All MSF members agree to honor the following principles:

MSF provides assistance to populations in distress, to victims of natural or man-made disasters, and to victims of armed conflict. They do so irrespective of gender, race, religion, creed, or political convictions.

MSF observes neutrality and impartiality in the name of universal medical ethics and the right to humanitarian assistance. MSF claims full and unhindered freedom in the exercise of its functions.

---

[11]Catholic Relief Services, *Bangladesh: Emergency Relief for Refugees*, November 2017, www.crs.org /file/12839/download?token=xbA2Em9v.

Members undertake to respect their professional code of ethics and to maintain complete independence from all political, economic, or religious powers.

As volunteers, members understand the risks and dangers of the assignments they carry out and make no claim for themselves or their assigns for any form of compensation other than that which the association might be able to afford them.[12]

This charter offers a simple, frank statement of the work MSF does. It seeks to save lives through humanitarian assistance, and it calls on its volunteers to give themselves selflessly to help whoever needs medical aid. In doing this, it rejects any affiliations that might minimize their capacity to offer that help impartially or to bear witness to the tragedies and atrocities its volunteers observe.

The one thing the charter does not offer is a reason for MSF's activities. Perhaps this is because MSF believes its motivation should be obvious. People are dying for lack of basic medical care. It is only reasonable that people of goodwill respond to this, especially people who are trained to care for those with medical problems. That they carry out this work in a voluntary and impartial way is enough to show they are sincere in wanting to improve people's standard of living.

The CRS mission statement (approved September 11, 2008), while broader in scope than the MSF charter because it deals with issues beyond medical assistance, offers a similar commitment to helping people in need. In doing so, though, it explains it is motivated by the teachings of Jesus:

> Catholic Relief Services carries out the commitment of the Bishops of the United States to assist the poor and vulnerable overseas. We are motivated by the Gospel of Jesus Christ to cherish, preserve and uphold the sacredness and dignity of all human life, foster charity

---

[12]"Charter," Médecins Sans Frontières, www.doctorswithoutborders.org/who-we-are/principles/charter.

and justice, and embody Catholic social and moral teaching as we
act to:

Promote human development by responding to major emer-
gencies, fighting disease and poverty, and nurturing peaceful and
just societies; and,

Serve Catholics in the United States as they live their faith in
solidarity with their brothers and sisters around the world.

As part of the universal mission of the Catholic Church, we work
with local, national and international Catholic institutions and
structures, as well as other organizations, to assist people on the
basis of need, not creed, race or nationality.[13]

Like the MSF charter, the CRS mission statement affirms that it will help
whoever is affected by a low standard of living regardless of their beliefs,
offering humanitarian aid especially to those who are struggling the most.
At the same time, it is clear about its Catholic identification and allegiance to Jesus Christ. This does not hinder but spurs its mandate to care
for others.

Between them, these organizations have saved tens of thousands of
people from illness, starvation, and unsafe living conditions. In doing
this, they have provided basic goods to consume, thereby increasing
standard of living and helping the needy take steps toward being integrated into the global consumer social structure. They are excellent
examples of humanitarian aid work, with each organization orches-
trating massive resources and sending workers into harsh conditions to
help those who stand in great need.[14] The fact that one organization

---

[13]"Mission Statement," Catholic Relief Services, September 11, 2008, www.crs.org/about
/mission-statement.

[14]The humanitarian commitment of both organizations is so similar that they face common dangers
while carrying out their missions. In 2015, for example, nine MSF workers were killed when a
hospital in Afghanistan was bombed. Shereena Qazi, "Airstrike Kills MSF Medical Staff in
Afghanistan," Al Jazeera, October 3, 2015, www.aljazeera.com/news/2015/10/3/air-strike-kills
-msf-medical-staff-in-afghanistan. In 2017, three CRS workers were killed by gunmen in
Afghanistan. Josh Smith and Mirwais Harooni, "Three Aid Workers Killed in Afghanistan:
Officials," Reuters, August 15, 2017, www.reuters.com/article/us-afghanistan-attack-idUSKC
N1AV1DG. For this reason, they were two of fourteen major international humanitarian

remains neutral in its allegiances and that the other identifies itself as Catholic makes no difference on the ground. A donor may choose to give to one of the organizations over the other because she is more attracted to what motivates the organization, but either way the donation will be used to improve needy people's standard of living. Both get the work done.

Given this similarity, can this humanitarian aid work, or any other effort to improve people's standard of living, be understood as bringing salvation? And, if so, can both secular and Christian organizations who help others be seen as participating in abundant life?

But Is It Salvation?

Salvation is not a term often used among secular organizations that work in humanitarian aid, likely because they see it as a religious term primarily connected to issues of spirituality and eternity, not addressing problems in this world. However, the word is not completely absent from their lexicon. Jeffrey Sachs, a professor at Columbia University and one of the foremost experts on international development, made this point in a report published in *The Economist* in 2002. Playing on the Bush administration's term *weapons of mass destruction* (WMD), he encouraged the United States to commit its people and funds to delivering "weapons of mass salvation" (WMS). He wrote,

> WMD can kill millions and their spread to dangerous hands needs to be opposed resolutely. WMS, in contrast, are the arsenal of life-saving vaccines, medicines and health interventions, emergency food aid and farming technologies that could avert literally millions of deaths each year in the wars against epidemic disease, drought and famine.[15]

---

organizations to commission a study on the risks their workers face in the field. "NGOs and Risk," Humanitarian Outcomes, 2019, www.humanitarianoutcomes.org/projects/ngos-and-risk.

[15]Jeffrey Sachs, "Special Report: Weapons of Mass Salvation," *The Economist*, October 26, 2002, 71.

Two years later an article ran in the *Canadian Medical Association Journal* titled "Weapons of Mass Salvation: Canada's Role in Improving the Health of the Global Poor," in which the authors argued for the Canadian government to increase its expenditures and efforts in combating major health crises worldwide.[16]

While the salvific outcome these articles describe is centered on saving people's lives in this world, the reference to salvation is nonetheless appropriate. As we have seen, the theological and biblical understanding of abundant life encompasses Christians sharing their gifts with others to save them from dangers in this world. Improving people's standard of living through humanitarian aid, especially helping those living in absolute poverty with no capacity to consume the necessities of life, fits with this. It grants salvation by helping the needy receive a portion of God's abundant life in the present world and by allowing the helpers to participate in abundant life through sharing with others.

There are no reasons Christians should reject or minimize this understanding of salvation. We can agree there are people who need to be rescued from a standard of living so low that it will at a minimum lead to social and economic isolation and maximally will lead to their deaths. Rescuing people from this not only fits with Birch's description of *shalom* in the previous chapter—as it overcomes chaos and provides for benevolence, relationality, and wholeness for those who receive it—but also tracks with the teachings and example of Jesus.

Jesus inaugurated God's kingdom on earth, demonstrating through his teaching and his compassionate acts of power that God's abundant life was overcoming the evil powers of this world. While improving people's standard of living was not Jesus' primary goal, he spent much of his ministry doing this. Jesus healed and fed people even as he taught them about

---

[16]Prabhat Jha, Bridget Stirling, and Arthur S. Slutsky, "Weapons of Mass Salvation: Canada's Role in Improving the Health of the Global Poor," *Canadian Medical Association Journal* 170, no. 1 (January 6, 2004): 66-67.

the kingdom of God. He also exhorted his followers to care for those in need. One of his most powerful messages on this point was the parable of the sheep and the goats.

"When the Son of Man comes in his glory, and all the angels with him, he will sit on his glorious throne. All the nations will be gathered before him, and he will separate the people one from another as a shepherd separates the sheep from the goats. He will put the sheep on his right and the goats on his left.

"Then the King will say to those on his right, 'Come, you who are blessed by my Father; take your inheritance, the kingdom prepared for you since the creation of the world. For I was hungry and you gave me something to eat, I was thirsty and you gave me something to drink, I was a stranger and you invited me in, I needed clothes and you clothed me, I was sick and you looked after me, I was in prison and you came to visit me.'

"Then the righteous will answer him, 'Lord, when did we see you hungry and feed you, or thirsty and give you something to drink? When did we see you a stranger and invite you in, or needing clothes and clothe you? When did we see you sick or in prison and go to visit you?'

"The King will reply, 'Truly I tell you, whatever you did for one of the least of these brothers and sisters of mine, you did for me.'

"Then he will say to those on his left, 'Depart from me, you who are cursed, into the eternal fire prepared for the devil and his angels. For I was hungry and you gave me nothing to eat, I was thirsty and you gave me nothing to drink, I was a stranger and you did not invite me in, I needed clothes and you did not clothe me, I was sick and in prison and you did not look after me.'

"They also will answer, 'Lord, when did we see you hungry or thirsty or a stranger or needing clothes or sick or in prison, and did not help you?'

"He will reply, 'Truly I tell you, whatever you did not do for one of the least of these, you did not do for me.'

"Then they will go away to eternal punishment, but the righteous to eternal life." (Matthew 25:31-46)

What is perhaps most compelling about this passage is that it emphasizes less how the humanitarian aid work provides salvation for those receiving it and more how it opens the door for those who are providing it to be saved. To be certain, those who are hungry, thirsty, naked, or lonely receive salvation from the immediate dangers of their low standard of living. At the same time, the king in the parable also judges that those who helped the needy are worthy of entering paradise. This teaching has had a deep impact on the church. CRS,[17] the International Orthodox Christian Charities (the primary humanitarian aid organization supported by the various Eastern Orthodox churches operating in the United States),[18] and a vast array of Protestant congregations all point to this parable as the foundational teaching of Jesus that spurs them to include humanitarian aid work as part of their missional outreach.

While theological perspectives among Christians vary on the intersection of faith and acts of compassion, all Christians recognize at least that God will hold people accountable for whether they have loved others, especially those in need. The book of James puts this pointedly:

What good is it, my brothers and sisters, if someone claims to have faith but has no deeds? Can such faith save them? Suppose a brother or a sister is without clothes and daily food. If one of you says to them, "Go in peace; keep warm and well fed," but does nothing about their physical needs, what good is it? In the same way, faith by itself, if it is not accompanied by action, is dead. (James 2:14-17)

---

[17]"CRS Upholds Catholic Teaching and Values," Catholic Relief Services, April 8, 2014, www.crs.org/media-center/crs-upholds-catholic-teaching-and-values.

[18]International Orthodox Christian Charities, *Strategic Plan, 2017–2021*, https://iocc.org/wp-content/uploads/2021/01/iocc-strategic-plan-2017-2021.pdf, 2.

Unless Christians love the needy by caring for their standard of living, James writes, their faith is unacceptable in the eyes of God. This points back to the missional aspect of participating in abundant life. It is not enough to receive the abundant life of God through faith in Christ. We must act on that faith by participating in abundant life, which means sharing it with others. In this sense, improving others' standard of living is doubly salvific for Christians. It brings salvation to the person being helped in this world and demonstrates that the Christians who do the helping are the faithful ones whom Jesus honors in the kingdom of God.

This dual salvation may seem suspect to those outside of the Christian faith. Do Christians really care about those in need, or are they just trying to get on God's good side by improving people's standard of living?

This question creates a false dichotomy. Even secular agencies recognize that doing good for others benefits those who do it. The Children's Defense Fund's document "Ending Child Poverty Now" (2015) offers an excellent example of how a secular organization frames its advocacy on behalf of children living in poverty in terms of the potential benefits everyone will reap from children being lifted from poverty:

> Reducing child poverty would yield incalculable benefits for millions of children and the country as a whole. . . . Eliminating child poverty between the prenatal years and age 5 would increase lifetime earnings between $53,000 and $100,000 per child, for a total lifetime benefit of $20 to $36 billion for all babies born in a given year. And we can never measure the countless innovations and discoveries that did not occur because children's potentials were stunted by poverty.[19]

Humanitarian aid always provides benefits for both those being helped and those who do the helping. When anyone improves the standard of living for those in need, they do something that benefits all, including

---

[19]Children's Defense Fund, "Ending Child Poverty Now," 2015, www.childrensdefense.org/wp-content/uploads/2018/06/Ending-Child-Poverty-Now.pdf.

themselves. Everyone benefits from an economy that has more people with more resources who can consume more goods and services.[20]

In this sense, there is a salvific element to humanitarian aid work regardless of the beliefs of those who provide it. God has set up the world in a way that rewards people for helping their neighbor in need. If this prompts some people to improve the standard of living for others, Christians should welcome that. At the same time, the Christian witness cannot stop there. Participating in abundant life is not motivated by self-interest!

One way Christians can demonstrate their interest in doing more than improving their own lot when improving people's standard of living is to follow the example of Jesus, who was willing to have his own life disrupted and interrupted so that people who had been ostracized could rejoin society.[21]

The first Christians took Jesus' practice to heart and invited people to join a community in which they shared their possessions with one another and cared for those in need as well as attended to the apostolic preaching of the gospel. This community made room for people regardless of race, ethnicity, sex, or social class. Later Christians in Rome and Byzantium were known both for their message of salvation and for their care of the sick, orphans, widows, and travelers, welcoming these needy people into their houses and monasteries.[22] Today, hospitality stands as one of the primary virtues that Christians are exhorted to foster, and it is practiced in a variety of ways on a local level, including neighborhood congregations banding together to provide winter shelters, soup kitchens, clothes cupboards, and pantries stocked with various

---

[20]The preceding two paragraphs are paraphrased from my book *Go! How to Become a Great Commission Congregation* (Nashville: Foundery Books, 2017), 53-54.

[21]For example, Jesus healed those with leprosy (Matthew 8:1-4; Mark 1:40-45; Luke 5:12-16; 17:11-19) who would have been thrust out of Israel's society as unclean (Leviticus 13:45-46). He likewise healed the woman with the issue of blood (Matthew 9:18-22; Mark 5:25-34; Luke 8:43-48), who likewise would have been shunned (Leviticus 15:19-27).

[22]Amy G. Oden, ed., *And You Welcomed Me: A Sourcebook on Hospitality and Early Christianity* (Nashville: Abingdon, 2001), 18-26.

necessities for families in need. In each of these cases, the goal is not only to improve people's standard of living through giving them access to what they cannot consume on their own but to provide a relationship with people in the community so those receiving the goods are not viewed as only second-class people because of their poverty. It is to provide life to their bodies and to their souls by treating them with dignity (something we will explore more in the next chapter on quality of life).

This willingness to endure a disrupted life on behalf of others is still insufficient for Christians, though. This is because participating in abundant life is not defined just by humanitarian actions but by the way the Holy Spirit transforms the way we think about the resources God makes available to us.

STEWARDSHIP

At the heart of Christians participating in abundant life through improving people's standard of living is the notion of stewardship. This is the idea that God has given everyone the ability to oversee a certain amount of God's abundance. As overseers, we have the freedom to use what God has given us in whatever way we want. However, at some point God will demand an accounting, and we will be judged based on what we have done with God's possessions.

Many of Jesus' parables dealt with stewardship, often describing the actions of servants that a king put in charge of his possessions while he was away. When the king returns, the servants are judged based on what they have done with the king's possessions. The parable most closely associated with improving people's standard of living features a servant that a king puts in charge of his entire household, including the other servants. This trusted servant must "give them [the other servants] their food at the proper time" (Matthew 24:45). If the servant uses the king's wealth to care for the other servants well, then the servant will be trusted with even greater possessions to care for (Matthew 24:47), but if the servant uses the king's possessions as if they were only for him while allowing the other servants to languish, the king will "cut him to pieces and assign him a place with the hypocrites, where there will be weeping and gnashing of teeth" (Matthew 24:51).

When linked with the parable of the sheep and goats, this parable confronts us with a dire warning. Those people who have greater access to income and goods in this world are not to claim these resources only for their enjoyment. They are to see what they have as a trust from God. Out of this trust, they are to provide for those who are needy. If they are faithful stewards, improving the standard of living for the "least of these," they will know God's fullest blessings. If they only seek to raise their personal standard of living higher, then God will strip away what they have, potentially including their share of abundant life.

For those who do not follow Jesus, this call to stewardship and the accountability it demands carries little weight. This is the primary difference between the type of salvation offered by those who provide humanitarian aid as Christians and those who do not. The former do so recognizing that they are caught up in a vast movement of God's abundant life that stretches from this world to the next (more on that in chapter six). The latter do so looking just for a better world in the here and now. This is not to condemn the latter group. They work to save people from a low standard of living with the best lights they have. However, it is to suggest that the secular vision may find its efforts snarled at times because of the way self-interest influences it.

A CRITIQUE

Two important critiques need to be addressed regarding the concept of standard of living, especially if we are to link it to abundant life. The first has been levied from secular contexts and speaks to the misguided ways humanitarian aid is administered globally. The second comes from Christians who would reject the idea of being allied to consumerism.

Critiquing humanitarian aid. The effectiveness of improving people's standard of living is easy to see on the micro level. When people are without food or shelter and they suddenly receive those things, we can observe that they are better off than they were. However, on the macro level the effectiveness is not as obvious. Organizations like the UN and World Bank declare that their work in international development (the systematic process of improving people's standard of living across the globe, especially in the poorest regions) has been highly successful. According to the World Bank Annual Score Card for 2017, for example, the percentage of the world's population living in extreme poverty (which the World Bank defines as under 1.90 USD per day) has dropped from 15.7 percent in 2010 to 10.7 percent in 2017. The goal was to bring this number down to 9 percent by 2020.[23]

While this is an improvement, some suggest that this work is not as successful as it seems and that there are problems it has not addressed. Paul Collier, in his book *The Bottom Billion*, is one of the leading voices on this matter. Collier states that while upward of four billion people were lifted from extreme poverty since the 1970s, one billion people are still left in this dire state and face a worsening standard of living.[24] The highly positive statistics cited by the World Bank and other large NGOs obfuscate this fact by globalizing growth rates.

Collier argues that these countries are cut off from the broader move toward prosperity by four "traps": civil war, dependence on natural resources as their only source of national income, being land-locked so that they are dependent on neighboring countries to give them access to international trade routes, and poor governance. Even if a country broke free from these traps, he claims that the globalized marketplace is difficult for small, poorly capitalized countries to enter as a trading partner. As such, they are likely to remain perpetually less developed than the richer countries unless the rich countries intervene to help.

---

[23]"Corporate Scorecards," World Bank/World Bank Group, October 2017, https://scorecard.world bankgroup.org/.

[24]Paul Collier, *The Bottom Billion: Why the Poorest Countries Are Failing and What Can Be Done About It* (New York: Oxford University Press, 2007), 9-10.

Humanitarian aid has traditionally been the way rich countries have intervened. However, by studying the impact of the four traps on the effect of aid in these countries, Collier uncovered an inconsistent record. At times aid helped, but often it had only a minimal effect or made things worse. These differing results arose from the rich countries (and the large NGOs they used to provide aid) being lax in their efforts. Rather than studying the traps that caused poverty and engaging in the hard work that would create the pathways for the poorest nations to reach affluence, they sought to give away aid in the easiest and quickest ways possible. This blunted the effectiveness of the aid and even allowed it to be wasted.[25]

Given this critique, it is essential to recognize that just as humanitarian aid meant to improve people's standard of living is not sufficient to address all the issues related to poverty, so it cannot be seen as a panacea leading to full salvation. At best, it saves people in immediate need and can help lay the groundwork for people to exit poverty in a more systemic way. However, it cannot do more without additional commitment and actions by those who have the resources to help. In Christian terms, it offers a taste of abundant life but nothing close to all of it.

This is a welcome critique. It reminds everyone who has the capacity to improve people's standard of living, regardless of their faith, that salvation is neither an easy nor an inexpensive activity. It requires that we share not only our wealth in a way that cares for others, but all our resources. Drawing on the image of the steward, it calls us to marshal our money, time, energy, influence, expertise, and every other asset or ability we control with others in mind. Only in doing this will we be participants in God's mission of providing abundant life for those we are helping even as we claim that abundant life more fully for ourselves. This is true not only in biblical terms but in secular economic terms. As Collier put it,

The problem matters, and not just to the billion people who are living and dying in fourteenth-century conditions. It matters to us.

---

[25]Collier, *Bottom Billion*, 123.

The twenty-first century world of material comfort, global travel, and economic interdependence will become increasingly vulnerable to these large islands of chaos. And it matters now.[26]

In offering aid that is more effective at helping those mired in poverty, we find some level of salvation both for them and for us. This is not salvation in the fullest sense for the needy or for us, but it is still an experience of abundant life we can share while we work for the common good.

Critiquing consumerism. The other critique is aimed at the logic underlying the concept of standard of living itself—namely, that it is grounded in consumerism. The notion of consumerism is so deeply related to unjust economic structures that linking it to participating in abundant life is problematic. Salvation should lift us out of a consumerist economy, not reinforce it!

The increasing influence of the marketplace in daily life has led to a growing literature about consumerism and consumption. The existence of *The Oxford Handbook of Political Consumption* is witness to this. According to the *Handbook*, mass consumption is a "material and cultural/ideological infrastructure" that promotes capitalist economic growth on a global scale by driving greater production of goods and services through encouraging greater consumption on the part of common people.[27] In doing this, people become viewed as "consumers," a label that pervades every aspect of their lives—economic, political, and even social.

While active consumers do drive a stronger economy, such that mass consumption is "widely celebrated and associated with norms of progress, success, and welfare,"[28] there are serious concerns about the cost associated with these benefits. We have already encountered the first concern in how people can be welcomed or rejected by peers based on whether

---

[26]Collier, *Bottom Billion*, 3-4.

[27]Magnus Boström and Mikael Klintman, "Mass Consumption and Political Consumerism," in *The Oxford Handbook of Political Consumerism*, ed. Magnus Boström, Michele Micheletti, and Peter Oosterveer (Oxford: Oxford University Press, 2018), 856.

[28]Boström and Klintman, "Mass Consumption and Political Consumerism," 857.

they have the ability to consume at least at a base level for the society in which they live. As the *Handbook* explains,

> In late modern society, the role of the consumer has become a necessity. One must be a consumer in order to participate as an actor in exchange on the market, to fulfil basic needs, to satisfy desires, to survive, and to live well. . . . The category of the consumer has grown as a social role.[29]

Even more concerning is that at the same time consumerism demands that everyone become a consumer to enjoy the benefits of a high standard of living, the very nature of consumerism denies some people that ability. To provide those who are wealthy with enough to consume, the consumer society needs a steady stream of affordable goods and services. This requires some people to become the cheap labor force that constructs and delivers the goods and services being consumed by the wealthy, denying these workers the income to consume at the level needed for them to be recognized as social equals with the wealthy.

Christian authors add another layer to this critique. Not only does consumerism hijack our human identities; it is idolatrous. According to Richard Bauckham, consumerism fulfills the four characteristics of idolatry:

1. It treats something that is relative as if it were absolute. In this case, it treats various goods and services as if they were able to fulfill us by their own power.

2. It prompts humans to believe that their desires are insatiable and must be satisfied continually by new goods and services, rather than teaching us that we must submit our desires to a greater good.

3. It enslaves us by demanding loyalty to the economic system that judges us based on our standard of living.

---

[29]Boström and Klintman, "Mass Consumption and Political Consumerism," 857.

4. It is deceitful, promising us an ever more enjoyable life while demanding greater servitude in order to afford the better life it says we will have.[30]

These are serious criticisms. Can the notion of standard of living remain ethically viable as a way of thinking about abundant life if consumerism disrupts how we relate to other people and to God?

It can. The danger of consumerism is in accepting it as a totalizing concept. When we allow consumerism, or any economic system, to become the metanarrative we use to explain how the world works, we run into trouble. That consumerism has become this sort of idol in political and economic circles is clear. That means we must be careful around it. We do not want to become servants of a consumerist society. At the same time, we need not abandon the tools of improving people's standard of living because of the dangers involved.

That consumerism is idolatrous does not change the fact that the needy must consume the necessities of life. Our resources rightly go to provide for this consumption on the part of the needy. As John Wesley explained it,

In the present state of mankind, though, [money] is an excellent gift of God, answering the noblest ends. In the hands of his children, it is food for the hungry, drink for the thirsty, raiment for the naked. It gives to the traveler and stranger where to lay his head. By it we may supply the place of an husband for a widow, and of a father to the fatherless; we may be a defence for the oppressed, a means of health for the sick, of ease to them that are in pain. It may be as eyes to the blind, as feet to the lame; yea a lifter up from the gates of death.[31]

While Wesley was speaking to an audience of his Methodist followers, his point is one that most people can accept in principle. We can use the

---

[30]Richard Bauckham, *The Bible in the Contemporary World: Hermeneutical Ventures* (Grand Rapids, MI: Eerdmans, 2015), 40-42.

[31]John Wesley, Sermon 50, "The Use of Money," §§16-24, in *Sermons II*, ed. Albert C. Outler, vol. 2 of *The Bicentennial Edition of the Works of John Wesley* (Nashville: Abingdon Press, 1976–), 268.

resources within our control to improve others' standard of living if we are wise. In doing this, we not only offer them God's gift of life as we help save them from their miserable situations, but we also receive salvation from the idolatry of consumerism that would trap us all. We move from the desiccated life of consumerism to participate in abundant life.

This is where the concept of stewardship comes back into play. Stewards must give an account to the ultimate owner of the goods and services entrusted to them. If we see ourselves as stewards who serve the marketplace, we will become little more than promoters of a subhuman identity for those we seek to help. Drawn inexorably by the logic of the consumerist market, we will only help them sufficiently to make them effective producers of the goods and services we desire to consume, whether those are shoes, lawn services, or just the warm feelings we get when we have been generous to those in need.

However, if we understand ourselves as stewards of Christ's abundant life, not just of physical resources, we will avoid this fate. We will not be unwitting pawns of the consumerist society but will be those who use the tool of humanitarian aid, among other forms of intervention, to save people from genuine dangers to their physical lives by improving their standard of living. We will do this because we believe God values them equally to us and has entrusted us with their care. Being entrusted with this care does not mean we are superior to them but rather that we are responsible to God for using resources in a way that honors them the way God honors them.

FROM GOOD DEEDS TO PARTICIPATING IN ABUNDANT LIFE

Based on the vast number of both large humanitarian aid agencies and local initiatives run by Christians to help the needy, most Christians already agree that improving people's standard of living is something they are supposed to do. Many congregations even see this work as their primary form of missional activity.[32] The issue is not whether we ought

---

[32]Mark R. Teasdale, "Quality of Life and Mission," *Missiology* 44, no. 3 (July 2016): 277.

to be involved with improving people's standard of living but whether we can articulate how this work is part of a larger witness to God's salvation through Jesus Christ.

We can if we express how we experience salvation as participating in abundant life. This shows our understanding of salvation is dynamic. Salvation is not just a gift received from God; it is a mission in which we join God in sharing life with others. It also expands our view of salvation to include how God provides for people to live in this world and the next. Combining these two ideas allows us to do more than just perform good deeds by helping those in need; it allows us to provide a full-orbed witness for the gospel as we improve other people's standard of living.

It also allows us to work alongside anyone who seeks to improve people's standard of living. Regardless of their creed, they are doing God's work by saving others at least in physical ways. Our role as Christians is not to condemn or question their work but to invite them to see how Jesus can supply not just the means for immediate lifesaving work but abundant life. We do this best by demonstrating the way we steward our resources in every facet of life, showing that we believe we are not superior benefactors who share our resources out of self-interest but that we share out of a desire to honor the dignity of our neighbors and to be honored by Jesus.

5

Saving Happiness

*What good is it for someone to gain the
whole world, yet forfeit their soul?*

MARK 8:36

JESUS SPOKE THE WORDS OF MARK 8:36 following a confrontation with Peter. After Jesus explained to his disciples that he would die soon, Peter challenged him, saying that such a thing could never be true. Jesus silenced Peter, then called his disciples to teach a larger point. Sometimes obeying God requires making sacrifices. This might be unpleasant, but it is worth it. What good would all the pleasures of life be if a person ended up in hell? Better to obey God and enter glory.

Those who are interested only in standard of living would struggle with Jesus' question. If all we care about is our standard of living, gaining the world might well be worth selling our souls! However, most people are not this crass. Even if they do not believe they have a soul to lose, they realize that even having an exceptionally high standard of living is not enough to have a good life. Someone could be opulently rich and still feel unfulfilled, unloved, and despondent. This points to the difference between standard of living and quality of life.

Standard of living refers to a person's capacity to consume. Quality of life points to the level of well-being a person feels. As critical as it is to improve people's standard of living so they can survive physically, there is an increasing recognition that addressing standard of living without quality of life is insufficient.

Nations, especially the wealthy nations that already have a high standard of living, have begun measuring their citizens' quality of life. The results of these studies prove that wealth alone is not enough to guarantee that people are living well. For example, the 2018 Human Development Report from the UN, which measures standard of living using the Human Development Index, ranked the United States as having the thirteenth highest standard of living in the world.[1] However, when citizens of the United States were asked to self-report on their sense of happiness for the World Happiness Report, the country ranked eighteenth.[2] Conversely, Costa Rica ranked sixty-third on the Human Development Index while coming in at thirteenth on the World Happiness Report. Clearly, wealth is no indicator of happiness.

The growing realization that improving people's standard of living will not necessarily improve their quality of life has led to a surge of research on quality of life during the past two decades. The research found that a major reason for poor quality of life in wealthy countries has to do with a pervasive sense of loneliness, especially among senior citizens and those working in heavily digital environments (which increased substantially during the pandemic quarantines). This loneliness leads to more than just feeling sad. It has been linked to greater risks of stress, inflammation, heart disease, type 2 diabetes, dementia, and suicidal thoughts.[3] Beyond the dangers caused by loneliness for individuals, there are economic implications. Vivek Murthy, surgeon general of the United States

---

[1] *Human Development Indices and Indicators: 2018 Statistical Update* (New York: United Nations Development Program, 2018), 22, http://hdr.undp.org/sites/default/files/2018_human_development_statistical_update.pdf.

[2] John F. Helliwell, Haifang Huang, Sun Wang, and Hugh Shiplett, "International Migration and World Happiness," in *World Happiness Report 2018*, ed. John F. Helliwell, Richard Layard, and Jeffrey D. Sachs (New York: Sustainable Development Solutions Network, 2018), 23, https://s3.amazonaws.com/happiness-report/2018/WHR_web.pdf.

[3] Jane E. Brody, "The Surprising Effects of Loneliness on Health," *New York Times*, December 11, 2017, www.nytimes.com/2017/12/11/well/mind/how-loneliness-affects-our-health.html?module=inline.

under both Presidents Obama and Biden, wrote an article in the *Harvard Business Review* dealing with the detrimental effects of loneliness in the modern workplace.[4]

The effects of loneliness are serious enough that governments are intervening. The highest-profile move came when the United Kingdom created a Minister of Loneliness in January 2018. The need for this was brought home to British politicians when they received the report of the Jo Cox Commission on Loneliness, which found that nine million British citizens were always or almost always lonely.[5] There was a clear sense that people needed to be saved from this loneliness.

The social isolation and stress brought about by the Covid-19 quarantines offer more insight into the need to be saved from a low quality of life. The British medical journal *The Lancet* published a review of multiple studies that measured the psychological impact of quarantine. Researchers found that

> most reviewed studies reported negative psychological effects including post-traumatic stress symptoms, confusion, and anger. Stressors included longer quarantine duration, infection fears, frustration, boredom, inadequate supplies, inadequate information, financial loss, and stigma.[6]

These studies were borne out by Dr. Elinore McCance-Katz, who served as an assistant secretary at the Department of Health and Human Services and the head of the Substance Abuse and Mental Health Administration, reporting that during the pandemic "there's more substance abuse, more overdoses, more domestic violence and neglect and abuse of children."[7]

---

[4]Brody, "Surprising Effects of Loneliness."

[5]Ceylan Yeginsu, "U.K. Appoints a Minister for Loneliness," *New York Times*, January 17, 2018, www.nytimes.com/2018/01/17/world/europe/uk-britain-loneliness.html.

[6]Samantha K. Brooks et al., "The Psychological Impact of Quarantine and How to Reduce It: Rapid Review of the Evidence," *The Lancet* 395, no. 10227 (March 14, 2020): 912-20.

[7]Jayne O'Donnell, "'Deaths of Despair': Coronavirus Pandemic Could Push Suicide, Drug Deaths as High as 150k, Study Says," *USA Today*, May 8, 2020, www.usatoday.com/story/news/health

Another report, copublished by the Well Being Trust and the Robert Graham Center,[8] stated that "a preventable surge of avoidable deaths from drugs, alcohol, and suicide is ahead of us if the country does not begin to invest in solutions that can help heal the nation's isolation, pain, and suffering."[9] Calling these deaths collectively "deaths of despair," this report used the correlation that occurred between unemployment and deaths of despair following the Great Recession in 2008 to determine how many likely additional deaths of despair would occur in the United States following the pandemic quarantine based on how extensive unemployment was and how quickly the economy recovered. For the years 2020–2029, the report determined that there would be minimally 27,644 additional deaths of despair (if there was a quick recovery and unemployment remained relatively low), up to a maximum of 154,037 additional deaths (if there was a slow recovery with higher unemployment).[10] While not calculating the numbers, the American Psychological Association also linked unemployment to suicide and mental health problems.[11]

Loneliness, isolation, stress, and other issues that lower quality of life are directly related to severe illness, self-destructive behavior, harming others, and death. They destroy people's ability to enjoy their lives in this world and close them to receiving the abundant life of God by making them feel hopeless. Participating in abundant life therefore must include improving people's quality of life. This requires more than just cheering up people when they feel sad. It demands a holistic approach to improving people's happiness and well-being. As those who follow the God

---

/2020/05/08/coronavirus-pandemic-boosts-suicide-alcohol-drug-death-predictions/308170 6001/.

[8]The Well Being Trust is a national foundation that addresses the mental, social, and spiritual health of the United States. The Robert Graham Center conducts policy studies on behalf of the American Academy of Family Physicians.

[9]Steve Petterson et al., *Projected Deaths of Despair During the Coronavirus Recession*, Well Being Trust, May 8, 2020, 4, https://wellbeingtrust.org/wp-content/uploads/2020/05/WBT_Deaths-of -Despair_COVID-19-FINAL-FINAL.pdf.

[10]Petterson et al., *Projected Deaths of Despair*, 11.

[11]Stephanie Pappas, "How Will People React to the New Financial Crisis?," *Monitor on Psychology* 51, no. 4 (May 4, 2020), www.apa.org/monitor/2020/06/covid-financial-crisis.

who cares specifically for the "brokenhearted" (Psalm 34:18; 109:16; 147:3; Isaiah 61:1 NRSV), our Christian witness is equipped to do this.

If You're Happy Can You Know It?

What is happiness?[12] Humanity has a long history of asking this question. Since happiness is subjective, it can be difficult to answer. However, there are some broad points of agreement.

Drawing their definitions from the ancient Greeks, social scientists state that happiness has two dimensions. The first is hedonic, sometimes referred to as an "affect." The second is eudaimonic, sometimes referred to as "contentment." The hedonic dimension of happiness is a transitory feeling that relates to immediate sensations of pleasure. Receiving recognition for a job well done, experiencing physical touch, or tasting gourmet food are all examples of this. The eudaimonic dimension of happiness is cognitive, relating to how someone understands their purpose in life and feels fulfilled as a human being when pursuing it. The combination of these two makes for what various researchers call a sense of happiness, well-being, or a high quality of life.[13]

While these two dimensions are both necessary for happiness, they are not equally important. This is because the hedonic dimension is known to adapt to people's usual level of happiness. Hedonic adaptation occurs when someone experiences an event that causes their sense of subjective well-being to go up or down. After a period of time, no matter how intense the experience was, their sense of well-being tends to revert to its initial baseline. While major life changes, such as getting married or

---

[12]A paper given at the Yale University conference on Happiness and Human Flourishing in December 2011 explained that a variety of terms have been used to refer to happiness by researchers, including "happiness, life satisfaction, and subjective well-being." Adam B. Cohen and Kathryn A. Johnson, "The Relation Between Religion and Well-Being," *Applied Research in Quality of Life* 12 (2017): 543. Experiencing any of these correlates to a positive quality of life. I will largely use the term *happiness* but will employ the others on occasion.

[13]Numerous articles in the *Encyclopedia of Quality of Life* provide much deeper insight into these definitions. See especially articles on eudaemonia, eudaimonic and hedonic happiness, happiness, and hedonic level of affect. A. C. Michalos, ed., *Encyclopedia of Quality of Life and Well-Being Research* (Dordrecht, The Netherlands: Springer, 2014).

experiencing a chronic health problem, can lead to a permanent shift in that baseline, there is at least a partial adaptation to the original sense of well-being insofar as people do not remain as high or low as they felt at the moment of the event.[14]

One reason that national wealth does not equate to national happiness is because hedonic adaptation occurs when a person's standard of living changes (a situation known as the Easterlin Paradox). Researchers have "not been able to show that changes in income or standard of living produce long-term (as opposed to transient) changes in S[ubjective] W[ell] B[eing]."[15] To the contrary, they have shown not only that an improved standard of living results in a fairly short-lived improvement in a person's quality of life but also that people's quality of life can suffer when they receive a higher standard of living. The Negative Endogenous Growth theory suggests that increasing one's standard of living beyond a certain point degrades the capacity for people to enjoy things that are not purchased through the marketplace, such as fresh air, sunshine, and friendship. So, being richer with greater consumption correlates negatively with a better quality of life.[16]

These insights should inform our Christian witness. As much as improving people's standard of living is necessary to literally save them from life-threatening deprivation, such work is not sufficient on its own. A fuller form of life is necessary, one that includes improving people's quality of life in a way that helps them develop lasting happiness. Recognizing this expands our understanding of what God offers through abundant life and how we can participate in abundant life through sharing it.

Poverty provides an excellent case study for this. It demonstrates not only how those living below the poverty line need to have both their

---

[14]Bruce Headley, "Hedonic Adaptation," in Michalos, *Encyclopedia of Quality of Life and Well-Being Research*, 2831-33.

[15]Headley, "Hedonic Adaptation," 2831.

[16]Francesco Sarracino and Małgorzata Mikucka, "Consume More, Work Longer, and Be Unhappy: Possible Social Roots of Economic Crisis?," *Applied Research in Quality of Life* 14 (2019): 59-84.

standard of living and quality of life improved but how working for that improvement can create the conditions for an entire society to be happier.

Implications for the poor and the good society. Advocates for overcoming poverty agree with the need to look beyond interventions that deal only with standard of living. The Webb Memorial Trust, established during the twentieth century to help bring about social reform in the United Kingdom on behalf of those living in poverty, concluded that dealing with poverty only in terms of improving poor people's capacity to consume was failing.[17] In part, this was because the notion of poverty had become highly politicized, such that people often disagreed as to who ought to receive aid and who should provide it.[18]

Instead of trying to tackle such a contentious issue, the trust determined that the best way forward was to discuss what it would take to develop a "good society." In doing this, they were able to involve a larger group of people in the conversation and engage them in a constructive process that included alleviating poverty but also moved beyond that. A survey of British citizens the trust commissioned through YouGov found that the top five traits chosen for a good society were social traits (fairness, a fair chance for all, freedom, safety, and security). Only the sixth was economic (well-paid work). The trust remarked in its report,

> For most people, the good life is not about having a lot of money; it is about having enough to pay their way and occasionally enjoy a few luxuries. Both having well-paid work and the absence of poverty are important, largely because they help people to live fuller lives. There was a general sense from the focus groups that material possessions matter less than community.[19]

Based on this common set of desires for a good society, the trust suggested that the best strategy was to form diverse groups of people and

---

[17]Barry Knight, *Rethinking Poverty: What Makes a Good Society?* (Bristol, England: Bristol University Press, 2017), 13.

[18]Knight, *Rethinking Poverty,* 15.

[19]Knight, *Rethinking Poverty,* 65, 67.

help them use their "moral imagination" to consider how to make this good society a reality. To test this idea, the trust gathered focus groups that included people from across the political spectrum. They found that, while people often began the conversation from a place of disagreement, having the opportunity to explain themselves in a way that uncovered their core concerns about life allowed them to find points of commonality in their hopes for the future. Further, it allowed participants to become more nuanced in their thinking because they could hear reasoned explanations for why people held perspectives different from theirs. As the report explained,

> This entails an inclusive process in which relevant people use divergent thinking to mold the society they have into the future they want. . . . [In doing this] we can find much that is common between us regardless of the outward complexion of our political views. While there is plurality, there is also scope for compromise.[20]

This hopeful view contends that most people, across political lines, can find common ground in seeking the common good. They do not have to give up their distinctiveness in this but can find ways to work together to improve the quality of life for both themselves and the people around them.

The outcome of this survey also shows that improving quality of life is not a linear process like improving standard of living. When improving standard of living, there is a clear need (a person or group of people does not have access to necessary goods and services) and solution (provision of those goods and services). Enacting the solution results in the people who are in need being saved from privation and the people who provide the necessary goods and services finding joy in sharing. While there is some mutuality in this, its structure is a benefactor-client relationship, with the latter improving the standard of living for the former.

Improving quality of life does not operate this way. When someone befriends a person who is lonely, the result is not just that the lonely

---

[20]Knight, *Rethinking Poverty*, 62, 65.

person now feels better. It is that a relationship is formed. This is a mutual process that improves the quality of life for both the one who initiates the friendship and the befriended. While the befriended person may have benefited more at the outset because the new friendship helped them overcome their loneliness, the quality of life for both is increased because both now enjoy a new relationship. Both enjoy the common good of being in a friendship.

This improvement in quality of life is increased even more when many people are brought together in a relationship through a community. It is further enhanced when that community has a dedicated purpose of working for the common good. Each person, regardless of how high their quality of life was individually when they entered the community, has that quality of life improved. As they build deeper connections with each other and enrich the society around them by working for the common good, their quality of life improves even more.

This simple example shows that the process of improving quality of life is better understood as a positive feedback loop than as a direct line, with each relationship and purposeful act toward the common good increasing the quality of life for everyone involved. The reverse is also true. As relationships are broken and as efforts toward the common good are halted, quality of life spirals downward. In its place, loneliness, isolation, and stress set in and become barriers to a better quality of life. The impact of poverty on people's quality of life is an example of this.

When an entire society is spiraling downward because the individuals in it are experiencing a low quality of life, the only way to reverse this trend is to introduce hope. This hope must be bigger than the relational brokenness people are experiencing. It also requires people who have been formed sufficiently in this hope so as not to be dismayed by the low quality of life in the society. Instead, they have an abundance of hope to share with others and enough compassion to take the initiative to share it.

Those of us who experience salvation as participating in abundant life meet these requirements. We have already received God's abundant life, which includes the assurance that God will supply all we need in this world and the next. This provides us with an inexhaustible supply of hope. In addition, as those called to participate in abundant life, we are inspired to love our neighbors by sharing the gifts God has given us with others. We are the compassionate, hope-filled people who can serve in God's mission by improving people's quality of life, and Jesus sets the example for how to do this.

JESUS THE COMMUNITY BUILDER

> Cardinal Glick: For example, the crucifix . . . this highly recognizable, yet wholly depressing image of our Lord crucified. Christ didn't come to Earth to give us the willies. . . . He came to help us out. He was a booster. And it is with that take on our Lord in mind that we've come up with a new, more inspiring sigil. . . . I give you . . . The Buddy Christ.[21]

At this point, some might be concerned that I am veering dangerously close to making the case in this quote from the movie *Dogma*. Far from it. I am not interested in defending the Buddy Christ. However, I do want to show that Jesus understood the work of improving people's quality of life as part of his ministry of sharing abundant life. He did this especially through forging relationships and building communities. So, while we rightly reject the glib "Buddy Christ," we can and should still sing "What a Friend We Have in Jesus" because of both the friendship Jesus offers to us and the relationships he helps us develop with others.

As described in the previous chapter, Jesus improved people's standard of living through healing. In doing this, he also improved people's quality of life by reconnecting them to the community around them. This was especially the case when Jesus healed someone who was unclean, such as lepers or the woman with the issue of blood. Their illnesses prevented them from relating to people lest they spread their ceremonial impurity

---

[21]*Dogma*, written and directed by Kevin Smith (Santa Monica, CA: Lionsgate Films, 1999).

to someone else. By healing them, he gave them the gift of healthy bodies and restored human interaction. He saved them from their sickness and from loneliness.

Dealing with a standard of living issue was not required for Jesus to improve someone's quality of life, however. Jesus saw relationships as important in their own right.

When Peter observed that he and the other disciples had sacrificed much to follow Jesus, Jesus acknowledged this and promised that God would honor what they had done:

> "Truly I tell you," Jesus replied, "no one who has left home or brothers or sisters or mother or father or children or fields for me and the gospel will fail to receive a hundred times as much in this present age: homes, brothers, sisters, mothers, children and fields— along with persecutions—and in the age to come eternal life." (Mark 10:29-30)

Jesus' response shows that he was more concerned with the sacrifice of quality of life than of standard of living. He realized that the disciples had to leave their homes, especially the people they loved. His response was that God would recompense this by providing new relationships. The disciples would be welcomed into new homes and have new brothers, sisters, mothers, and children. In other words, they would be knit into a new community. This was so important to Jesus that he dedicated most of his answer to promising this community, nearly overshadowing the brief mention of eternal life at the end of the passage. However, the fact that he connected God's provision of community in this world with the promise of future glory is notable. It shows that Jesus saw both as part of the abundant life he brought.

Jesus made a similar comment when he was told his family was waiting for him outside the place he was teaching. Seizing the opportunity, he explained that he came to build a community of those who honored God. "'Who are my mother and my brothers?' he asked. Then he looked at those seated in a circle around him and said, 'Here are my mother and my brothers! Whoever does God's will is my brother and sister and mother'" (Mark 3:33-35). Again, in this situation Jesus spoke in the present tense. He was not offering a glorious community in the future but rather real relationships in the present as part of the abundant life he offered.

Jesus practiced what he preached about community. He made a point of connecting with people through parties, dinners, and regular worship at the synagogues. He welcomed those he met along the way to join him. Many he encountered did so joyfully, such as Bartimaeus (Mark 10:52). He called the disciples, inviting them to be in a relationship with him and each other.

Perhaps the best-known account of Jesus forging a relationship with someone is his encounter with the Samaritan woman at the well. Recorded in John 4:1-42, the story depicts Jesus sitting by a well as his disciples go to buy food. While he is there, a woman from the local Samaritan village comes to draw water. What ensues is one of the longest of Jesus' dialogues recorded in the Bible. During this conversation, we hear both the voices of Jesus and the Samaritan woman as Jesus invites the woman to consider a new way of understanding life. The woman is skeptical at first but eventually comes to recognize Jesus as a unique messenger from God, even running back to her village to share about him. Based on this, the people invite Jesus to stay with them. He agrees to do this, teaching among them for two days.

This interaction is noteworthy for many reasons, including the social and religious conventions that Jesus defies to hold this conversation. Two of these are that Jews and Samaritans would not relate to one another, the former believing the latter to be unclean, and that men would not converse with women. He could have ignored the woman, preferring his solitude since he was tired (John 4:6). The religious and social contexts would have made that reasonable, and the woman would have expected it. Yet he spoke to her, beginning the conversation by acknowledging that she had something that he did not: water to drink (John 4:7). Having

likely surprised her both by taking the initiative to speak and by recognizing a gift she could give to him, she responded. From this a relationship
grew between them in which Jesus offered the woman reasons to
trust him.

Jesus did not just want to establish a single relationship between
himself and the woman, however. He wanted to develop a community.
To do this, he facilitated the woman engaging with her village in a new
way. The woman was so impressed with Jesus that she ran to the village
to explain how amazing Jesus was (John 4:29). This resulted in the villagers coming to meet Jesus themselves and then inviting him and his
disciples to stay with them for two days. The story ends with the woman
and the villagers in a conversation in which the people tell her that they
found her testimony about Jesus to be true (John 4:39-42). As Jesus
leaves the village, he leaves everyone with an improved quality of life
because of their relationship with him and the new ways that the people
in the village relate to each other as a community.

Community organizers who read this passage add another element to
what Jesus offered the woman and the village: leadership development.
Jesus recognized the woman as a potential leader in her village and used
his conversation with her to prompt her to lead the villagers to faith.[22]
This offered a further improvement in their quality of life because this
leadership would guide the villagers toward more purposeful lives.

By intentionally laying aside social strictures to build a relationship
with the woman, Jesus created the opportunity for both the woman and
her village to form a community of believers. In doing this, Jesus improved the quality of life of everyone involved, initiating the upward
spiral by first improving the woman's quality of life and then the entire
village's as the woman forged stronger relationships with and among
the villagers. Anticipating our next chapter, he also showed how

---

[22]My thanks to the Reverend Dr. Angela Cowser, associate dean of Black Church Studies and Doctor
of Ministry Programs and associate professor of Black Church Studies at Louisville Presbyterian
Theological Seminary, who pointed out this element of the story.

naturally improving people's quality of life can lead to offering them eternal life.

The community of the baptized. The early Christians recognized how Jesus brought life to people by creating communities and followed his example. In the book of Acts, the Holy Spirit descended on the small group of those who believed in the resurrection of Jesus and enabled them to create a community in a polyglot crowd by allowing them to speak different languages (Acts 2:4). Empowered to share the good news of God's salvation through Jesus with everyone, the Christians, led by the apostle Peter, exhorted people to repent of their sins and be baptized (Acts 2:38). Those who were convinced by Peter's witness did this and joined the community of believers (Acts 2:41).

Baptism was more than a ritual of repentance. It was the entryway to entering the new community with a new way of living together. It was a way that both addressed standard of living and quality of life through how those within it related to each other:

> They devoted themselves to the apostles' teaching and to fellowship, to the breaking of bread and to prayer. Everyone was filled with awe at the many wonders and signs performed by the apostles. All the believers were together and had everything in common. They sold property and possessions to give to anyone who had need. Every day they continued to meet together in the temple courts. They broke bread in their homes and ate together with glad and sincere hearts, praising God and enjoying the favor of all the people. And the Lord added to their number daily those who were being saved. (Acts 2:42-47)

The verb tense used by the author is noteworthy. The people who joined the community of Christians were not those who "had been saved" when they made their decision to follow Jesus or who "would be saved" by going to heaven in the future, but those who "were being saved." Part of their salvation was participation in the community itself. Their experience of salvation meant participating in abundant life as part of a community of Christians. Likewise, there is no differentiation between those who had followed Jesus from the beginning or those who had just joined the community of Christians at Pentecost. All were blessed by the increasing community with its purposeful way of living.

Christians will point to the uniqueness of the apostolic message of Jesus' life, death, and resurrection as grounding this community. This is because, while being in any community allows us to receive a portion of God's abundant life, a fuller experience of the abundant life God offers us comes from being in a community gathered around Jesus that both receives God's goodness and shares in God's mission. This is the heart of how improving people's quality of life intersects with participating in abundant life. Abundant life is not something we participate in only as individuals. It is something that we grow into with others. While each of us is called individually to follow Jesus Christ, it is by coming together with others who likewise follow Jesus that we more fully experience the abundant life Christ offers us. As John Wesley expressed it, "'Holy solitaries' is a phrase no more consistent with the gospel than holy adulterers. The gospel of Christ knows of no religion, but social; no holiness but social holiness."[23]

THE GREATER GOOD

While Christians have a unique community of mission that welcomes people into abundant life, many of the practical ways we can intervene specifically to improve others' quality of life are the same as those used by all people of goodwill. We can especially do this through helping people increase their happiness.

Both the insights of the social scientists and surveys we have already reviewed, as well as teachings about happiness from antiquity, link

---

[23]John Wesley and Charles Wesley, "Hymns and Sacred Poems" (1738), ¶ 5, in *The Works of John Wesley*, ed. Thomas Jackson, 14 vols., CD-ROM edition (Albany, OR: Ages Software, 1996, 1997), 14:437.

increased happiness with lives dedicated to a greater good than just fulfilling personal desires. In *The Republic* Plato depicts Socrates explaining how general happiness can arise within a country only when people stop seeking individual happiness and work for the common good of the state. This is especially true for the "guardians," who are the philosophers entrusted with enacting and enforcing the laws.

> We must consider whether in appointing our guardians we would look to their greatest happiness individually, or whether this principle of happiness does not rather reside in the State as a whole. But if the latter be the truth, then the guardians and auxiliaries, and all others equally with them, must be compelled or induced to do their own work in the best way. And thus the whole State will grow up in a noble order, and the several classes will receive the proportion of happiness which nature assigns to them.[24]

While we disagree with Socrates's assumption that people are assigned specific roles and social classes by nature that limit their ability to experience happiness, his larger point stands. A higher quality of life is achieved when everyone looks beyond their personal happiness to the greater good of the society in which they live. When people seek to do their best for one another (to love their neighbor as themselves, to put it in the words of Jesus), they all gain a happier life from that.

Aristotle gives happiness an even higher position than Socrates. At the beginning of his *Nicomachean Ethics*, Aristotle declares, "Of all the good things to be done, what is the highest[?] Most people, I should think, agree about what it is called, since both the masses and sophisticated people call it happiness, understanding being happy as equivalent to living well and acting well."[25] Having established happiness as the ultimate good for people to achieve, he then lays out his understanding of what true happiness entails. In doing this, he uses the Greek word

---

[24]Plato, *The Republic*, trans. Benjamin Jowett (London: The Clarendon Press, 1908), book 4, 276.
[25]Aristotle, *Nicomachean Ethics*, trans. Roger Crisp (New York: Cambridge University Press, 2000), 5.

eudaimonia, from which modern researchers developed the eudaimonic dimension of happiness.

Aristotle agrees in principle with Socrates that happiness arises from everyone serving their particular purpose in society, although he arrives at the conclusion from a different direction. For Aristotle, happiness is an action of the soul rather than as an external blessing humans seek. Because of this, he understands happiness as arising from within the human being through virtuous action. He writes, "The happy person is the one who, adequately furnished with external goods, engages in activities in accordance with complete virtue, not for just any period of time but over a complete life."[26]

Acknowledging that people must first have a basic standard of living in order to attain a better quality of life, Aristotle states that each person's virtuous activities will differ. Some will be more prosaic, like a carpenter, and some more elegant, like a mathematician.[27] These virtuous activities are useful to those beyond the person performing them. The carpenter finds happiness not only in building well but also when others live and work in the buildings he constructed. The mathematician finds happiness not only in working through geometric proofs but also when others benefit from the beautiful architecture that derives from that geometric work. Both the individual and the society increase in happiness when individuals contribute to the common good in a virtuous way.

The classical notion that happiness and virtue are connected was so strong that it survived two thousand years to inform the Enlightenment. Enlightenment political philosophers held that one of the chief aims of government should be to protect people's ability to achieve happiness. John Locke, like Aristotle, argued that the desire for true happiness was the ultimate aim for humanity. According to Locke, seeking after true happiness (which relates to the eudaimonic dimension of happiness) restrains our desires for immediate pleasure (which relate to the

---

[26]Aristotle, *Nicomachean Ethics*, 18.
[27]Aristotle, *Nicomachean Ethics*, 12-13.

hedonic dimension of happiness). This restraint does not quash our desires for pleasure but brings them into alignment with what will be most fulfilling for us:

> As therefore, the highest perfection of intellectual nature lies in a careful and constant pursuit of true and solid happiness; so the care of ourselves, that we mistake not imaginary for real happiness, is the necessary foundation of our liberty. The stronger ties we have to an unalterable pursuit of happiness in general, which is our greatest good, and which, as such, our desires always follow, the more we are free from any necessary determination of our will to any particular action, and from a necessary compliance with our desire, set upon any particular, and then appearing preferable good, till we have duly examined whether it has a tendency to, or be inconsistent with, our real happiness.[28]

Since individuals would be able to reach personal fulfillment only through seeking after true happiness, Locke contended that people should be free to do this. He emphasized this point in the marginal note he made to the above quote: "The necessity of pursuing true Happiness [is] the Foundation of Liberty."[29]

Pursuing true happiness is foundational not only for the individual, who is set free to live a fulfilling life rather than following one unsatisfying pleasure after another, but also for the state. By guarding its citizens' ability to strive for a happy (and thereby more virtuous) life, the state fosters a society in which its citizens can grow into their full potential individually as well as in relationship to one another. This strengthens the state by filling it with happy and virtuous citizens who will be more willing to support and defend the state because of the good life it allows them to pursue. Inspired by this idea, Thomas Jefferson famously wrote in the Preamble to the Declaration of Independence for the United States

---

[28]John Locke, *An Essay Concerning Human Understanding* (London: Clarendon Press, 1894), 1:348.
[29]Locke, *Essay Concerning Human Understanding*, 1:348.

of America that all people "are endowed by their Creator with certain unalienable Rights, that among these are Life, Liberty, and the pursuit of Happiness."

These insights are not unique to political philosophy. They are also found in the work of Thomas Aquinas. Aquinas dedicated five questions, each with eight articles, to happiness in the *Summa Theologica*. Drawing from Aristotle,[30] Aquinas came to a similar conclusion as Locke. Happiness is the ultimate good that humans aspire to, and because of that, the desire for happiness orders how humans use their will. He wrote, "The will tends naturally to its last end; for every man naturally wills happiness: and all other desires are caused by this natural desire; since whatever a man wills, he wills on account of the end."[31]

Aquinas went further, positing two levels of happiness: perfect happiness and imperfect happiness. Perfect happiness is the ultimate end of human existence and consists in the intellectual contemplation of God. Imperfect happiness is experienced in this body through the senses.[32] While imperfect happiness is less important, this does not mean that Aquinas rejected it. Rather, recognizing that the bodily resurrection of Jesus Christ means that the physical body is valued by God and will be transformed into something glorious, Aquinas acknowledged that "happiness does not consist in bodily good as its object: but bodily good can add a certain charm and perfection to Happiness."[33] Likewise, Aquinas believed that basic bodily needs (standard of living) must be met in order for people to focus on the perfect happiness (quality of life) that contemplating God offers:

> For imperfect happiness, such as can be had in this life, external
> goods are necessary, not as belonging to the essence of happiness,

---

[30]Aquinas even cites Aristotle's *Nicomachean Ethics* relating to happiness; see Thomas Aquinas, *Summa Theologica*, trans. Fathers of the English Dominican Province (Claremont, CA: Coyote Canyon Press, 2006), I, Q. 62, Art. 1; I-II, Q. 3, Art. 2; and I-II, Q. 4, Art. 7.

[31]Aquinas, *Summa Theologica*, I, Q. 60, Art. 2.

[32]Aquinas, *Summa Theologica*, I-II, Q. 3, Art. 3.

[33]Aquinas, *Summa Theologica*, I-II, Q. 4, Art. 6.

but by serving as instruments to happiness, which consists in an operation of virtue, as stated in [Aristotle's *Nicomachean*] *Ethic*. For man needs in this life, the necessaries of the body, both for the operation of contemplative virtue, and for the operation of active virtue, for which latter he needs also many other things by means of which to perform its operations.[34]

While Aquinas did not deal with the role of the state in relation to happiness, he did hold that human relationships are connected to happiness. He addressed this by asking whether the fellowship of friends is necessary for happiness. Initially, he answered that friendship is only necessary for imperfect happiness, since humans find their perfect happiness in God alone:

If we speak of the happiness of this life, the happy man needs friends, as the Philosopher [Aristotle] says, not, indeed, to make use of them, since he suffices himself; nor to delight in them, since he possesses perfect delight in the operation of virtue; but for the purpose of a good operation, viz. that he may do good to them; that he may delight in seeing them do good; and again that he may be helped by them in his good work. For in order that man may do well, whether in the works of the active life, or in those of the contemplative life, he needs the fellowship of friends. But if we speak of perfect Happiness which will be in our heavenly Fatherland, the fellowship of friends is not essential to Happiness; since man has the entire fulness of his perfection in God.[35]

Having made this point, Aquinas equivocated. While insisting that happiness comes from God alone, he found that participating in a community supports this perfect happiness. Drawing from Augustine, he wrote, "But the fellowship of friends conduces to the well-being of Happiness." A few paragraphs later, in considering how love of neighbor flows from our love of God, he stated, "Friendship is, as it were,

---

[34]Aquinas, *Summa Theologica*, I-II, Q. 4, Art. 7.
[35]Aquinas, *Summa Theologica*, I-II, Q. 4, Art. 8.

concomitant with perfect Happiness."[36] So, for Aquinas, developing a community is indispensable for raising people's quality of life in this world. It is also something that is conducive to enjoying the perfect quality of life people gain when they enter God's eternal glory.

While some would disregard Aquinas's claim that the eudaimonic dimension of happiness is attainable only through the contemplation of God, they may be more open to his broader point, which agrees with the teachings of Socrates, Aristotle, and Locke. To attain happiness is equivalent to being fulfilled as a human being or, put another way, to experiencing the greatest goodness available for humans. As we pursue that happiness, we are saved from loneliness and purposelessness, obtaining a more abundant life, if not the fullness of abundant life. The alternative is an unfulfilled life, in which we wrongly order our desires by seeking after only those pleasures that quickly pass away. In the pursuit of those pleasures, we turn inward and fail to recognize our calling to participate in the lives of those around us, shrinking our lives rather than expanding them.

We gain even greater happiness by sharing what we have with others. We do this best through being part of a community that cares for the common good.

AN ORGANIZED, VIRTUOUS COMMUNITY

A community, according to Mark Lau Branson and Juan F. Martínez, is a voluntary gathering composed of individuals who have a "shared hope and imagination" and often cooperate in "side-by-side activities rooted in shared meanings and goals."[37] By participating in a community, people can have a strong sense of belonging to something bigger than themselves. They also are given a framework that can make them virtuous.

Both the philosopher Alasdair MacIntyre and leadership expert Walter Fluker argue that communities have the power to define and instill

---

[36]Aquinas, *Summa Theologica*, I-II, Q. 4, Art. 8.
[37]Mark Lau Branson and Juan F. Martínez, *Churches, Cultures and Leadership: A Practical Theology of Congregations and Ethnicities* (Downers Grove, IL: IVP Academic, 2011), 83.

virtues in those who belong to them. MacIntyre states that communities do this by weaving narratives that give people a sense of what values are worth maintaining in the face of resistance.[38] They tell the stories of great heroes who held fast to the community's values even under great adversity, presenting these heroes as role models for others in the community to emulate.

For Fluker, these community narratives convey an ethical foundation that forms leaders who have the capacity to reform the "systemworlds" that determine how power and resources are distributed.[39] Fluker offers the examples of Howard Thurman and Martin Luther King Jr. as leaders who were raised in the African American community, which inculcated them with an alternative set of values from what the dominant American culture promulgated during their lifetimes. Thanks to being nurtured in these values, they were able to challenge the dominant cultural values. In place of the bigotry and racism they encountered, which lowered people's quality of life, they offered the vision of a "beloved community" that would welcome all comers and so increase everyone's quality of life.[40]

Fluker's examples show how virtuous communities offer abundant life on several levels. First, the African American community saved both Thurman and King from accepting the dominant racist values of their time, raising them to become leaders who operated out of an alternative ethic. In return, both Thurman and King enlivened the African American community by helping secure rights and liberties they had long been denied. More than this, their work offered a new vision of life to all Americans by reframing how Americans understood the way they should relate to one another. They presented Americans with the vision of a community that does not allow for a high quality of life for some to be

---

[38]Alasdair MacIntyre, "The Virtues, the Unity of a Human Life, and the Concept of a Tradition," chap. 15 in *After Virtue: A Study in Moral Theory* (Notre Dame, IN: University of Notre Dame Press, 1984), 126-27.

[39]Walter Earl Fluker, *Ethical Leadership: The Quest for Character, Civility, and Community* (Minneapolis: Fortress Press, 2009), chap. 6.

[40]Fluker, *Ethical Leadership*, chap. 1.

predicated on a lower quality of life for others but rather one that provides all people equal liberty to pursue happiness. To be sure, the life provided in all these situations was only partial, and in the case of race relations in the United States, there is still much chaos and sin that must be defeated. Notwithstanding, the power of the African American community to raise ethical leaders who could become agents of salvation by bringing life to others is real.

Is it possible to replicate this sort of community that will raise up new leaders for today? Community organizing is one way to create a community with an intentional focus on leadership development.

A primary practice of community organizing is the relational meeting. These are brief meetings in which the organizer takes the time to meet people and learn about them, especially what passions they have and how they might grow as leaders. The goal of the meeting is not to enlist people to work for a cause but rather to build individual relationships and to identify how a person might be activated to improve the community. When a problem arises that requires action, the community organizer can call on the people with whom they have built relationships to step forward as leaders. Usually, these problems relate to an injustice that is harming people's standard of living. The community organizer and other leaders advocate for those affected, seeking to rectify this situation.

In doing this, community organizing offers life in two ways. It improves the quality of life of those who are drawn into a meaningful community and developed as leaders. It also unleashes those leaders in a way that improves the standard of living for those in need. If, as Jesus did with the Samaritan woman, it also invites people into eternal life, then it can be a full means of participating in abundant life for Christians.

RELATIONAL HAPPINESS

Formal community organizing is not necessary to help people experience abundant life through improving their quality of life, though. As Aquinas pointed out, it can also be done through simple friendship.

Aquinas argued that having friends improves people's happiness in this world and helps them more fully appreciate the perfect happiness of heaven. While scientists cannot test the claim about heaven, studies have demonstrated the correlation between friendship and happiness. The peer-reviewed *Journal of Happiness Studies* (yes, this does exist, and yes, it has serious scholarship in it!) has run several articles in which social scientists have tested this relationship. This included a series of articles by Melikşah Demir, a leading researcher on the psychology of happiness and friendship. These found that friendships lead to greater reported happiness for people of all personality types, especially when those friendships include a sense of companionship (enjoying spending time with one another) and self-validation (feeling listened to and supported).[41]

In a follow-up study, which sought to explore the connection between the hedonic dimension of happiness and friendship, Demir concluded that friendship makes us happy because it fulfills basic psychological needs. He wrote,

One reason why the quality of friendships is related to happiness is because friendship experiences provide a context where basic needs are satisfied. Friendships involve spending time together in a variety of activities such as talking about daily events, providing support and disclosing personal information. That is, individuals are likely to experience several provisions in their friendships to varying degrees. It seems reasonable to suggest that experiencing these provisions in close relationships might help the individual feel comfortable to freely express themselves, feel and act in a competent manner and experience a strong bond in their friendships, which in turn predict happiness.[42]

---

[41]Melikşah Demir and Lesley A. Weitekamp, "I Am So Happy 'Cause Today I Found My Friend: Friendship and Personality as Predictors of Happiness," *Journal of Happiness Studies* 8 (2007): 181-211.

[42]Melikşah Demir and Metin Özdemir, "Friendship, Need Satisfaction and Happiness," *Journal of Happiness Studies* 11 (2010): 255-56.

On a more intimate level, one article reported on the impact of people's perception of their marital relationship on their overall sense of well-being. Not only did a higher marital relationship quality correlate to a greater sense of well-being, but if one spouse had a higher sense of well-being, that could break through hedonic adaptation and permanently lift the other spouse's sense of well-being.[43]

Another article examined how even short-term, bounded times of coaching could improve well-being. In an experiment run with middle school students, it was found that just five one-hour sessions in which students were exposed to practices of how to "(1) conceptualize clear goals; (2) produce numerous range of pathways to attainment; (3) summon the mental energy to maintain the goal pursuit; and (4) reframe seemingly insurmountable obstacles as challenges to be overcome" led to substantial increases in the students' hope, life satisfaction, and self-worth. These increases were sustained even eighteen months after the sessions.[44]

The results of these studies show that improving quality of life in lasting ways does not require complex interventions or technical know-how. Rather, it can occur through simply taking time to be involved with other people in a way that meets them as they are, pays attention to them, listens to them, supports them, and shares our best with them. This is something we can do with our spouses or existing friends over the course of years as well as something we can offer through brief, daily interactions. All people are capable of this, Christians especially so because of the happiness we already have in Christ.

Christians, and other people of faith, have an additional tool to help improve people's quality of life because most of us already participate in

---

[43]Kristin Gustavson et al., "Life Satisfaction in Close Relationships: Findings from a Longitudinal Study," *Journal of Happiness Studies* 17 (2016): 1293-1311.

[44]Susana C. Marques, Shane J. Lopez, and J. L. Pais-Ribeiro, "'Building Hope for the Future': A Program to Foster Strengths in Middle-School Students," *Journal of Happiness Studies* 12 (2011): 139-52.

congregations.[45] By befriending people and welcoming them into our congregations, we can offer all the psychological benefits of friendship. In addition, if we are intentional about articulating our faith, our congregations can provide a context where everyone in them, whether a longtime member or a new visitor, can be formed in virtue (à la MacIntyre and Fluker).

Christian communities have a particular power to meet the needs of those who are lonely and isolated because we believe that God desires all people to have abundant life. This means that the church should provide a place that welcomes all people, not discriminating on the basis of sociological categories or political litmus tests that are often used to divide people. It is enough that God has worked through Jesus Christ to bring abundant life to all people. The church needs no more authorization than this to welcome everyone equally.

Beth Seversen, who has studied the congregations most effective at attracting and retaining young adults in the United States, suggests that congregations not only can but must welcome those who are not yet Christians to share in the congregation's community and service, even investing resources in them and providing them with leadership development before they decide to follow Christ. This creates the positive feedback loop of giving those who have been invited a sense of being cared for by the community and of allowing them to respond to that care by contributing to the community's well-being through their service.[46] This care and service reinforce each other in a way that both improves the quality of life for those invited into the congregation and shapes their identities. The result is that the same qualities which attracted the people

---

[45]"Many religious groups, such as Judaism, Catholicism, and Hinduism, emphasize integration into a religious community as a valuable aspect of religion in and of itself, and not merely as a byproduct of the more intrinsic aspects of religion. This could result in greater social support, which is a known correlate of greater well-being." Cohen and Johnson, "Relation Between Religion and Well-Being," 6.

[46]Beth Seversen, *Not Done Yet: Reaching and Keeping Unchurched Emerging Adults* (Downers Grove, IL: InterVarsity Press, 2020), 96.

to accept the invitation into the community also retain them and bring them to conversion.[47]

The intentional creation of these sorts of communities is transformative not only for the people who enter them but for the congregations that embody them. These congregations "pull away from anything that reminds them of excess, bureaucracy, institutionalism, consumerism, and even colonial tendencies," replacing all this with being "incredibly hospitable and openhearted to unchurched people . . . [and] at the same time purposefully engaging cultural outgroups."[48] Here we see the mutuality of improving people's quality of life as God blesses both those whose quality of life is low and those who reach out to improve others' quality of life.

Reaching this ideal will not be easy for many congregations. Seversen acknowledges that it will take intentional work on the part of the pastor to reshape a congregation's culture around evangelism, leading the congregation to those outside the Christian faith as much as those outside the Christian faith to the congregation.[49] For many congregations, it is about realizing that they exist not for their own growth but for receiving and sharing the abundant life of Christ with others. This demands moving beyond thinking only about what will benefit the "church family" and what sorts of people are the most likely demographic to improve numbers and giving (usually upper middle-class, White, nuclear families) and instead considering who the people are that most need to be loved by a community. Congregations may balk at this, pointing to how it will disrupt their comfort. The response to this is that their comfort is disrupting their ability to participate in abundant life. Participating in abundant life comes not when we are comfortable but when we extend ourselves in mission to love God and neighbor, giving freely of what we have received to bless others and to support the common good.

---

[47]Seversen, *Not Done Yet*, 153-58, 210.

[48]Seversen, *Not Done Yet*, 204.

[49]Seversen, *Not Done Yet*, 122.

THE HAPPY GIVER

Quality of life is a complex and multifaceted concept that connects with every aspect of how we experience our daily lives. It speaks to our sense of happiness, which itself entails both immediate pleasure and a long-lasting sense of meaning and contentedness. Far from being a surface-level concern, measuring quality of life has become a major area of study for researchers and governments. This is because having a happy citizenry is just as essential to maintaining a healthy society as having a well-functioning economy; indeed the former is necessary to sustain the latter. Philosophers and theologians throughout history have consistently made this point, and social scientists are confirming it today.

The primary force undermining people's quality of life in the developed world today is the pervasiveness of loneliness, isolation, and stress. Cut off from social contact, people find themselves suffering from a variety of physical and psychological maladies, some leading to death. This has sent governments scrambling to gather more information on quality of life so they can address what has become a major public health issue. They seek to save their citizens from the chaos and darkness of loneliness. They desire to find salvation for their population by improving their quality of life.

The salvation the nations search for is not something that technology or programming can fix, though. As social scientists, philosophers, and theologians across the millennia have concluded, improving someone's quality of life requires people who are willing to give to others. Only when someone is willing to give their time, energy, and attention, as Jesus did with the Samaritan woman, can the people that person reaches out to find improvement in their quality of life. This quality of life increases even more when people integrate with a community that calls them to live for a greater good than just satisfying their personal desires.

The prophet Malachi understood this. When the people of Israel complained that God was not granting them a sufficient quality of life, he reminded them that a nation would be blessed with the happiness of God only if it first gave:

> You are cursed with a curse, for you are robbing me—the whole nation of you! Bring the full tithe into the storehouse, so that there may be food in my house, and thus put me to the test, says the Lord of hosts; see if I will not open the windows of heaven for you and pour down for you an overflowing blessing. I will rebuke the locust for you, so that it will not destroy the produce of your soil; and your vine in the field shall not be barren, says the Lord of hosts. Then all nations will count you happy, for you will be a land of delight, says the Lord of hosts. (Malachi 3:9-12 NRSV)

Both the prophets and Jesus made it clear that giving to God happened not only through tithes and offerings but through caring for those in need. And when a nation is full of people who give freely of themselves to build relationships and form communities, an upward spiral of improved quality of life occurs for everyone. However, someone needs to step forward and start that upward movement. Christians who participate in the abundant life of God should be those initiators by giving of themselves to enter friendships and form communities as well as by reshaping their existing congregations to become communities working for the common good of those outside the Christian faith.

Jesus and the early church provide a reproducible example of how to forge these kinds of relationships, both in short-term settings and in long-term communities. In doing this, they demonstrated that participating in abundant life allows Christians to be conduits through which God can save people by improving their quality of life. This serves both the common good and lays the foundation for engaging people with the message of eternal life.

6

Eternal Life

*For God so loved the world that he gave his
only Son, so that everyone who believes in him
may not perish but may have eternal life.*

JOHN 3:16 NRSV

IF YOU SEARCH "MOST POPULAR BIBLE VERSE," John 3:16 ranks at or near the top of almost every list. It adorns shirts, soars across interstate billboards, appears on signs held up at football games, is memorized by children in Sunday school classes, and is routinely heard on the lips of evangelists and preachers.

There is good reason for this popularity. Spoken by Jesus in simple and accessible language, the verse lays out a distinctively Christian narrative: (1) God exists and loves all of creation, with a special focus on humanity. (2) Humanity faces death. (3) God is unwilling for humanity to die, so sends God's only Son to save them. (4) Humanity needs to believe in the Son to be saved from death. (5) Salvation entails eternal life.

This narrative is simple and powerful, providing insight into the nature of God, what God does to make salvation available, and the way we should respond to receive salvation. Many of the evangelistic methods used to share the Christian faith with those unfamiliar with it follow this narrative (e.g., the Romans Road, the Four Spiritual Laws, the Four

Circles). What could be better than a God who loves us to the point of sending God's only Son so that we might live eternally?

There is something better: a God who loves us enough to send God's only Son so we can live abundantly. This abundant life includes the entire narrative in John 3:16 as well as the rest of the scriptural witness about salvation. The abundant life of God flows through us now as well as into eternity, unbroken by physical death. In addition, we do not just receive abundant life; we participate in it. We are invited both to believe in the Son and to join in his mission to bring abundant life to all creation. This mission involves improving people's standard of living and quality of life as well as sharing the message of eternal life through Jesus. Each saves people from the forces of chaos, sin, and death that afflict them, and each offers God's blessing of life.

While this holistic view of salvation is affirmed biblically and theologically, we need to address a potential concern. Bringing together the three concepts of standard of living, quality of life, and eternal life as constitutive parts of abundant life runs against the grain of how many Christians think about salvation.

As Alan Hirsch and Mark Nelson contend in their book *Reframation*, in which they call on Christians to reframe the gospel in winsome and creative ways to attract a world that is desperate for the life it brings, many Christians have reduced the gospel by limiting the ways we believe God can be encountered and communicated with as well as by restricting our understanding of the human condition.[1] Drawing from the work of L. Callid Keefe-Perry, they claim this reduction has resulted in

- Ossified doctrines; where ideas are believed but not lived, and faith degenerates into religious ideology.

- Wooden proclamations; where little resonates with the people beyond (and inside) the church, and theological boredom becomes the order of the day.

---

[1] Alan Hirsch and Mark Nelson, *Reframation: Seeing God, People, and Mission Through Reenchanted Frames* (Los Angeles: 100 Movements Publishing, 2019), 50.

- Empty doxologies; where ritualized religion replaces true worship, with no relationship to the eternal and universal perspective.

- Legalistic ethics; where discipleship is reduced to religious moralism, and shame and guilt replace freedom.[2]

Christians tend to reduce salvation to one of two things based on where they are on the theological spectrum: helping those in need (usually among liberal Christians) or saving souls (usually among conservative Christians). Both views fall short of what Jesus offered. There is a spiritual aspect of salvation that deals with personal sin and judgment that the liberals often downplay, and there is a physical aspect of salvation that deals with people's bodies and material needs, including social justice, that the conservatives often minimize.

The concepts of standard of living and quality of life sync well with the physical aspects of salvation, giving us nuanced ways to discuss them, especially in a secular culture. These concepts also offer a framework for how people of goodwill, whether secular, Christian, or adherents of another religion, can work toward the common good. This includes feeding the hungry, sheltering the homeless, tending the sick, befriending the lonely, and providing a community for the isolated. Anyone working for people to be saved in these ways is offering a portion of the abundant life of Christ whether they acknowledge God or not. As Jesus told his disciples when they saw others unaffiliated with their group who were casting out demons, "Whoever is not against us is for us" (Mark 9:40 NRSV). To miss this or reject it in the name of promoting eternal life is problematic because it ignores the scriptural witness for salvation to include rescuing people from the perils of this world, especially as seen in Jesus' ministry. It also forecloses on the potential of being a witness for Christ in a way that the secular world can understand, especially those in the secular world who already demonstrate compassion and care for people in need.

---

[2]L. Callid Keefe-Perry, *Way to Water: A Theopoetics Primer* (Eugene, OR: Cascade, 2014), 7, quoted in Hirsch and Nelson, *Reframation*, 53.

Offering a portion of abundant life is not enough, though. As important as improving standard of living and quality of life is in expressing our love of neighbor and allowing us to work for the common good with others, it reduces God's gift of salvation to just humanitarian aid if the Christian narrative of eternal life is not included.

The Christian witness must show that the kingdom of God is active in the world even as the chaos and darkness of want, deprivation, loneliness, and injustice swirl. It cannot do this fully unless it declares that the abundant life of the kingdom will claim final victory by extending from this world into eternity, where chaos will be no more. Apart from sharing this, Christians are neither participating as fully as they could in abundant life nor extending abundant life in all the ways God desires people to receive it. This is why Jesus also said, "Whoever is not with me is against me, and whoever does not gather with me scatters" (Matthew 12:30 NRSV). Christians can appreciate and work with others of goodwill, but they cannot allow their mission of serving Christ to be coopted, minimized, or diluted by agendas that are not Christ's. To stay faithful in this mission requires Christians to keep eternity in view as they participate in abundant life.

This brings us back to John 3:16. This verse makes it clear that abundant life extends beyond the physical world, presenting Jesus Christ as the unique way God provided to save people so that they will share in God's goodness eternally rather than be condemned by the judgment of God. Much of the New Testament expands on this.

GOD'S JUDGMENT AND SALVATION THROUGH JESUS

Jesus taught about God's final judgment more than anyone else in the Bible. We have already seen some of these teachings in the parables about stewardship when the owner returns to judge the servants on their use of the owner's goods. In the parable of the sheep and the goats (Matthew 25:31-46), Jesus explained that the judgment will take place "when the Son of Man comes in his glory, and all the angels with him." At that time, "he will sit on the throne of his glory. All the nations will be gathered before him, and he will separate people one from another" (Matthew 25:31-32 NRSV). Other parables describe the separation of people at the final judgment, such as the parable of the weeds (Matthew 13:24-30) and the parable of the net (Matthew 13:47-49).

There is real danger for those who are judged as unfaithful. Five times Jesus says that the unfaithful characters in his parables will be sent to a place of "weeping and gnashing of teeth" away from the happiness of the Lord and the Lord's faithful ones (Matthew 8:12; 13:42; 13:50; 22:13; 24:51 NRSV).

His most explicit description of what happens at the final judgment is in the parable of the rich man and Lazarus (Luke 16:19-31). Jesus tells of how a rich man and a beggar, named Lazarus, both die. The rich man is judged as unfaithful because he refused to share his high standard of living with Lazarus. As a result, he is tormented in a fiery place that Jesus calls "Hades." Lazarus is judged as righteous for faithfully enduring his painfully low standard of living and is comforted in a paradise Jesus calls "Abraham's bosom." The rich man is able to see Lazarus being comforted. Desperate for help, he calls out to ask Lazarus to ease his pain. He is answered by the Jewish patriarch Abraham, who says, "Between you and us a great chasm has been fixed, so that those who might want to pass from here to you cannot do so, and no one can cross from there to us" (Luke 16:26 NRSV).

Jesus was even blunter about final punishment in other teachings that were not parables. When preparing his disciples for their evangelistic work, he told them directly, "Do not fear those who kill the body but cannot kill the soul; rather fear him who can destroy both soul and body in hell" (Matthew 10:28 NRSV).

Jesus understood punishment after death to be a real possibility at the final judgment. This punishment was something to be avoided at all costs. There is a need to be saved from it!

The authors of the rest of the New Testament picked up on this theme. Peter warns that "the present heavens and earth are reserved for fire, being kept for the day of judgment and destruction of the ungodly" (2 Peter 3:7). The author of Hebrews flatly states, "People are destined to die once, and after that to face judgment" (Hebrews 9:27). John does not describe the judgment, but he assures the faithful, "We will have confidence on the day of judgment" (1 John 4:17).

Given that the Bible teaches there is a postmortem judgment and that it comes with the potential for terrible suffering, a reasonable question to ask is what God uses as the basis for that judgment. The biblical material offers a two-part answer to this. In doing so, it connects eternal life to participating in Christ's abundant life on earth.

Saved by faith in Jesus Christ. God's first basis for judgment is the foundational teaching of the Protestant church: that a person must have faith in Jesus Christ to be saved eternally. The reason for this is that all people have sinned and are therefore unable to enter God's holy presence. This means that at the judgment all people must be separated from God eternally. However, because God loves people, God is unwilling to accept this situation. To rectify it, God sent Jesus Christ to forgive human sin and reconcile humans back to God. Because of this forgiveness, people can be judged worthy of entering eternal glory. The book of Hebrews develops this idea of salvation, pointing to the death of Jesus on the cross as the means by which God offers forgiveness and assurance when facing the final judgment: "So Christ was sacrificed once to take away the sins of many; and he will appear a second time, not to bear sin, but to bring salvation to those who are waiting for him" (Hebrews 9:28).

While there are different theological explanations for how this forgiveness takes effect, most theological traditions agree that people should respond to this gracious offer of forgiveness through having faith in Jesus Christ. Through faith they are assured of eternal salvation because they no longer have any sin held against them. In the book of Acts, Peter made this point in the sermon he gave during the Festival of Pentecost, exhorting the crowd to "repent and be baptized, every one of you, in the name of Jesus Christ for the forgiveness of your sins" (Acts 2:38). Later he insisted on the uniqueness of Jesus in offering salvation when he told the Jewish leaders, "Salvation is found in no one else, for there is no other name under heaven given to mankind by which we must be saved" (Acts 4:12).

In his letters, Paul explained that it was impossible to gain God's forgiveness through any human effort. No level of obedience to the Jewish law nor performance of good deeds would efface sin and grant salvation. Paul preached in Pisidian Antioch, "Therefore, my friends, I want you to know that through Jesus the forgiveness of sins is proclaimed to you. Through him everyone who believes is set free from every sin, a justification you were not able to obtain under the law of Moses" (Acts 13:38-39).

Paul expanded on this teaching in the book of Romans. He argued that the salvation offered by Jesus was available to all people as the remedy God provided for the common sentence of eternal condemnation because of human sin:

> Consequently, just as one trespass resulted in condemnation for all people, so also one righteous act resulted in justification and life for all people. For just as through the disobedience of the one man the many were made sinners, so also through the obedience of the one man the many will be made righteous . . . so that, just as sin reigned in death, so also grace might reign through righteousness to bring eternal life through Jesus Christ our Lord. (Romans 5:18-21)

More than this, Paul argued that the resurrection of Jesus meant humans were saved from death itself. Not only would they be freed from eternal condemnation because of their sin, but they would be freed from death to rise again and share in the glory of God. He wrote, "Now if we died with Christ, we believe that we will also live with him" (Romans 6:8). This was also his theme in 1 Corinthians 15:52-57:

> For the trumpet will sound, the dead will be raised imperishable, and we will be changed. For the perishable must clothe itself with the imperishable, and the mortal with immortality. When the

perishable has been clothed with the imperishable, and the mortal with immortality, then the saying that is written will come true: "Death has been swallowed up in victory." . . . Thanks be to God! He gives us the victory through our Lord Jesus Christ.

Consequently, Paul exhorted his readers to declare their faith in Jesus, which would allow them to participate in eternal salvation, including forgiveness from sin and eternal life that overcomes death itself: "If you declare with your mouth, 'Jesus is Lord,' and believe in your heart that God raised him from the dead, you will be saved. For it is with your heart that you believe and are justified, and it is with your mouth that you profess your faith and are saved" (Romans 10:9-10).

Judged on good deeds. God's first basis for judgment is grounded firmly in God's gracious work through Jesus Christ. Paul's teaching especially makes it clear that eternal salvation cannot be earned through any good works, only by receiving through faith the gracious forgiveness and eternal life that Jesus made available by his crucifixion and resurrection.

However, this is not the final word on judgment after death in the Bible. While faith in Jesus is the cornerstone of eternal salvation, God still judges how we have lived. As Jesus explained in the Sermon on the Mount, "Not everyone who says to me, 'Lord, Lord,' will enter the kingdom of heaven, but only the one who does the will of my Father who is in heaven" (Matthew 7:21). We not only must have received the abundant life of God, we must have participated in it by being part of Jesus' mission.

The early church took this seriously. In his description of the judgment, Paul explains that God will review how we have lived. Paul believes that faith in Jesus is sufficient to save us but that we can still face loss if we have not been faithful in our living:

For no one can lay any foundation other than the one already laid, which is Jesus Christ. If anyone builds on this foundation using gold, silver, costly stones, wood, hay or straw, their work will be shown for what it is, because the Day will bring it to light. It will be revealed with fire, and the fire will test the quality of each person's work. If what has been built survives, the builder will receive a reward. If it is burned up, the builder will suffer loss but yet will be saved—even though only as one escaping through the flames. (1 Corinthians 3:11-15)

He repeated this idea in 2 Corinthians 5:10, "For we must all appear before the judgment seat of Christ, so that each of us may receive what is due us for the things done while in the body, whether good or bad."

This idea is made even more explicitly in the book of Revelation. Following the final defeat of evil and in preparation for populating the new heaven and the new earth, the dead are judged by God:

Then I saw a great white throne and him who was seated on it. The earth and the heavens fled from his presence, and there was no place for them. And I saw the dead, great and small, standing before the throne, and books were opened. Another book was opened, which is the book of life. The dead were judged according to what they had done as recorded in the books. The sea gave up the dead that were in it, and death and Hades gave up the dead that were in them, and each person was judged according to what they had done. Then death and Hades were thrown into the lake of fire. The lake of fire is the second death. Anyone whose name was not found written in the book of life was thrown into the lake of fire. (Revelation 20:11-15)

The two distinct kinds of books point to the two different bases for judgment. The "book of life" is the book that records the names of those who have placed their faith in Jesus Christ. Being inscribed in this book saves people from eternal fire. The other books provide a record of every-thing each person has done. It is not clear if the second set of books can overrule the "book of life," but it is clear that even those whose names are found in the "book of life" must also give a reckoning for what is found in the second set of books.

Neither Paul nor the book of Revelation describes how God judges the way people lived. Presumably, though, both fall in line with what Jesus called the "greatest commandment" (Matthew 22:38-39). Did people love God and their neighbors?

In his parables about stewardship, Jesus provided concrete examples of how to love God and neighbor by declaring that God would judge people based on how they used the resources God made available to them. If they squandered those resources on themselves or refused to use the resources at all, they would be condemned. If they used the resources to care for others, they would be welcomed into God's joy. This is what happens to the servants who are characters in the stewardship parables.

We need to be clear at this point. The servants are being judged on their stewardship of the resources available to them, not on their belief. The servants in Jesus' parables were already part of the owner's household, and the owner already trusted them completely with his resources. They are being judged not on whether they had accepted the lordship of the owner but on whether they were faithful in their service to the owner by how they cared for others with the owner's resources. Three parables in Matthew 25 demonstrate this: (1) Both the wise and the foolish virgins were in the service of the bridegroom, but only the wise ones are judged worthy of entering the feast because they used their time well to remain a blessing to the wedding party, while the foolish ones did not (Matthew 25:1-13). (2) All three of the servants the master left with money were trusted stewards in the household, but only the two who used their money well were invited into their master's joy. The third servant had the master's trust stripped from him and was cast out of the household (Matthew 25:14-30). (3) Both the sheep and the goats call the Son of Man "Lord," but only the sheep who cared for the "least of these" are invited to enter eternal life, while the goats are cursed with eternal punishment (Matthew 25:31-46).

This dual judgment explicitly connects eternal life to the life God offers on earth. Those who desire to enter eternal life not only need to have faith in Jesus Christ to receive forgiveness for their sins but also need to care for the needs of others in the present world. The abundant life of the disciples of Jesus Christ is bound up in sharing God's abundant life with others physically.

A transformed life. This brief biblical survey shows that Jesus and the early church believed abundant life starts in this world and reaches into eternity. This is not an equivocation about eternity. That God offers salvation in the present, physical world in no way precludes or diminishes God continuing to offer salvation that overcomes the grave in a new heaven and a new earth. God's promise of abundant life is meant to encompass both. Both are acts of God's grace that require humans to receive them, and both require people to steward them well.

In addition, all aspects of abundant life are premised on grace. This is just as true whether God is offering forgiveness for the sinner, companionship for the lonely, or food for the starving. God offers each as an act of love to save the person from the forces of chaos and death that beset them. However, God only offers; the person must choose to trust God and receive the gift. The sinner could refuse forgiveness, the lonely person could reject the proffered friendship, and the starving person could refuse to eat. This rejection might seem absurd in light of such obvious needs, but that does not mean God removes the option for people to reject the gifts God gives. To receive at least part of the abundant life of God means to accept God's gracious offer of a blessed standard of living, quality of life, and/or eternal life. To receive the fullness of life is to recognize God as the source of all these good gifts made available through Jesus Christ.

However, just receiving these gifts of life is not enough, since receiving the gifts of life does not mean that we are transformed by them. We could eat and simply be satisfied after becoming full, neither offering gratitude for the meal nor considering if we need to do something to avoid going hungry again, much less becoming compassionate toward other people who are hungry. We could take our friendships for granted and not reciprocate the care we receive from our friends. We could rest secure that we are forgiven for our past sins and become morally lax in how we live in the present. That we received the saving gifts does not guarantee we remain participants in the abundant life we received.

To participate in abundant life, we must share our physical and spiritual gifts by improving others' standard of living and quality of life as well as by inviting people to receive eternal life. For those that accept the gifts we offer, we welcome them to join us as we participate in the abundant life of God together, experiencing salvation as we share God's goodness with others. In all these ways we are acting as good stewards by using the good things God has entrusted to us for the care of others, including both the gospel and our physical resources. Put another way, we become faithful disciples of Jesus Christ who are part of Christ's mission to make new disciples.

This, then, is what participating in abundant life looks like: God graciously offers us the good gifts of an abundant life both now and into eternity through Jesus Christ, we receive and enjoy these gifts and the salvation they bring, we steward these gifts well by sharing them with others, and we invite those we share the gifts with to join us in sharing the good gifts of salvation with yet others. All of this is done in the name of Jesus Christ, through whom God provides abundant life.

What about secular agencies who seek to improve people's standard of living and quality of life? Are they also disciples of Jesus Christ because they are sharing the physical aspects of abundant life with others and sometimes invite the people they help to join them in their work? No. As we remarked earlier, someone has to decide intentionally to become a disciple of Jesus Christ. There are no anonymous Christians.

However, insofar as there are people who enjoy a portion of the abundant life of God in this world, who share those gifts by meeting people's needs, and who encourage those they help to go and help others, we can recognize kindred spirits. Such people, like the teacher of the law who at least understood that the chief commandments were to love God and neighbor, are not far from the kingdom of God (Mark 12:34). We should not deride their lack of explicit faith in Jesus Christ. Rather, we should encourage them in the work they are doing, even partnering with them as agents of life in this world. We should also invite them to consider the eternal life Jesus offers us alongside of the standard of living and quality of life they already know, enjoy, and invite others to share. We will be more successful in offering this if we approach them as those who already are on the path of salvation rather than as those who are far from it.

While we make this offer, we know not everyone will accept it. Given this, is there a limit to how far Christians can work alongside secular agencies? The logic of Christian salvation is not a secular logic. How can Christians retain their distinctive teaching about eternal salvation through Jesus Christ while operating in a secular culture that only recognizes the need for physical salvation?

DISTINCTIVENESS AND THE NEED FOR AN AFFIRMATION

We have already seen in previous chapters the problem of accepting secular models and concepts as a basis for salvation. Doing so can lead Christians to become purveyors of oppressive economic or political systems rather than those who participate in an abundant life that transcends human authorities and agendas. Specifically, we saw that improving standard of living in a way that perpetuates consumerism runs counter to the ethic of justice and abundance for all people. To do this would vitiate the logic of the abundant life we seek to offer. For this reason, we cannot uncritically adopt the ideas promoted by secular organizations.

Unfortunately, the uncritical acceptance of secular ideas about salvation has become commonplace among many Christian congregations today. Because they lack a clear understanding of what salvation is, they choose outreach activities based on what is most interesting to them without the ability to articulate how those activities are different from what a civic organization might do, much less how they relate to salvation.[3] Not surprisingly, these types of activities often seek to improve people's standard of living and quality of life. When Faith Communities Today, a division of the Hartford Seminary Institute for Religion Research, investigated the most common missional activities supported by both evangelical and conciliar Protestant congregations, it found they were (in order from least to greatest) direct cash assistance to the needy, food pantries or soup kitchens, clothing ministries (including thrift shops and closets), crisis hotlines, and health ministries (including hospitals and nursing homes).[4]

As life-giving as these activities are, they fall short of the abundant life offered through Jesus Christ. As a result, Bryan Stone argues that Christian congregations end up becoming unwitting agents of unjust systems by accepting the benefactor-client paradigm that assumes those with greater resources are superior to those with fewer resources (a concern we have already seen that runs counter to promoting quality of life). Ironically, this is even more likely when religious humanitarian work is welcomed by secular powers. According to Stone,

> Religious institutions now become essentially privatized arms of . . .
> "the great global machine" and are dedicated to the administration
> of a particular set of "spiritual" goods and services. . . . The church
> thus privatized, spiritualized, and depoliticized ends up "helping"
> the colonized adjust themselves to empire instead of enacting an
> embodied critique of the system that produced their colonization
> in the first place. This help might come in the form of pieties and
> spiritualities or it might come in the form of material and cultural

---

[3]Heather Lear, Teaching and Research Fellow at the Foundation for Evangelism, found that this lack of ability to articulate the salvific importance of the outreach work a congregation was doing was even prevalent among the most numerically successful congregations in her denomination. Heather Heinzman Lear, "Reclaiming Evangelism: Evaluating the Effect of Evangelism in Selected United Methodist Congregations on Fulfilling the Denominational Mission to Make Disciples" (DMin diss., Garrett-Evangelical Theological Seminary, 2015), 77.

[4]My thanks to my DMin advisee, Corey Nelson, in finding this information. Corey Nelson, "The Local Church Discerning Mission Partners: Exploring Best Practices for Choosing Faithful and Effective Mission Strategies" (DMin diss., Garrett-Evangelical Theological Seminary, 2014), 22.

institutions and support, such as schools, hospitals, and social charities. But empire remains intact. When the domesticated church does "go public," it tends to do so within the social imagination of the empire, on its terms, and within its discourse.[5]

Stone's answer to this is for the church to become a community marked by an alternative ethics, politics, and economics, all different from what the secular world offers. While I am sympathetic to the kind of community he wants to create, I believe his recommendation ultimately fails. This is because he claims that the ethical structure of the church should be "something like a virtue ethics where the end is internal to the means—where virtuous action is its own reward."[6] This logic forces us to reject working within or alongside of secular agencies because doing so would taint our means and, therefore, our ends. As I have tried to show, I believe that working alongside people who are secular in their beliefs is not only acceptable but a way of participating in abundant life in a secular context.

While the church should embody ethics that are not the same as the secular world's, it can do this only if it first clarifies how it is distinctive from secularism. In doing this, it knows what boundaries it must maintain as it partners with secular agencies and operates within a secular framework. Missionaries offer us helpful insights on this, as their work calls them to serve in settings where the logic of the gospel is not present.

Lesslie Newbigin. Lesslie Newbigin, best known today as a prescient missiologist whose work launched the missional church school of thought, spent much of his career as a missionary in India. In 1964 he gave a series of lectures on secularism and Christianity that were later compiled into a book titled *Honest Religion for Secular Man*.

---

[5]Bryan Stone, *Evangelism After Pluralism: The Ethics of Christian Witness* (Grand Rapids, MI: Baker Academic, 2018), 33, 35.
[6]Stone, *Evangelism After Pluralism*, 18.

He begins the book by acknowledging that secularism is on the move, spreading across the globe and transforming all that it touches.[7] Not all these transformations were bad from Newbigin's perspective. Quoting fellow missionary and theologian John MacKay, Newbigin stated, "In many of its aspects, secular civilization is the disinterested pursuit of human welfare."[8] He expanded on this point:

> An essential ingredient to the process of secularization is the dissemination of the belief that the conditions of human life can be radically bettered . . . that it is possible to create a new order of human existence in which poverty, disease and illiteracy are banished and all men can enjoy the privileges of what are called the developed nations.[9]

This belief that human life can be improved is important to Newbigin because it has the power to break the negative impact of religion. He saw this in how secular thinking around human development began overcoming the religious resistance of the Asian cultures to improving their standard of living:

> It cannot be denied that the main thrust of the teaching of the ancient Asian religions has been away from a concern to change the world. Their dominant teaching has been that the wise man is he who seeks to be content with the world, to be released from attachment to it, but not to seek to change it. The idea of total welfare for all men as a goal to be pursued within history is foreign to the Asian religions. . . . [Instead] it is part of the western invasion of the last few centuries.[10]

He also described the changes in standard of living and quality of life occurring in India through secular efforts:

---

[7]Lesslie Newbigin, *Honest Religion for Secular Man* (Philadelphia: Westminster Press, 1966), 11.
[8]Newbigin, *Honest Religion for Secular Man*, 9.
[9]Newbigin, *Honest Religion for Secular Man*, 26-27.
[10]Newbigin, *Honest Religion for Secular Man*, 27.

The process of secularization in India is accomplishing the kind of changes in patterns of human living for which Christian missionaries fought with such a stubborn perseverance a century and a half ago—the abolition of untouchability, of the dowry system, of temple prostitution, the spread of education and medical service, and so on.[11]

According to Newbigin, secularism was an aid to the missionary enterprise in Asia! Moreover, Newbigin's view of the positive influence of secularism was not reserved for Asia and its religions. "I have seen enough to know how powerful a source of evil religion can be. Nor is it necessary to go outside of Europe to have that demonstration."[12] He criticized the way that the European church had become too comfortable during Christendom and credited secularization with helping end this both by dissolving the easy relationship between European society and the church and by forcing the church to recognize the impact missionary activities can have throughout the world:

The process of secularization, by which the sacral unity of the Christendom society has been broken and the Church has been set in a new relation with society, has been the pre-condition for the recovery of a biblical, that is to say, a pre-Constantinian, understanding of the Church as a missionary community. On the other hand, the experience of western missionaries working in pagan sacral societies and finding themselves, to their own surprise, to be agents of secularization, has helped older Churches of the western world to recover a missionary doctrine of the Church itself.[13]

Given all of this, Newbigin advocated for the church to engage with the process of secularization, especially in how it worked for the development of people's standard of living and quality of life. Such

---

[11]Newbigin, *Honest Religion for Secular Man*, 17.
[12]Newbigin, *Honest Religion for Secular Man*, 9.
[13]Newbigin, *Honest Religion for Secular Man*, 104.

development was "a secularized form of the biblical idea of the Kingdom of God. It is rooted in the understanding of human history as the sphere of God's redeeming acts."[14]

As enthusiastic as Newbigin was about the way secularism had forced religious people around the world out of their complacency, prompting Christians to be missionary again and other religions to accept activities that could improve the standard of living and quality of life for their adherents, he also was aware of its potential dangers. Most concerning was the possibility of the secular enterprise collapsing because it had no foundation. Granted, secularism had helped tear down the negative influences of religion to bring about human development, but did it have something in which to ground that development? Did it have an affirmation for why it engaged in this development after negating the problematic beliefs that had held back that work? "The negation will become self-destructive if it does not rest upon an affirmation," Newbigin warned.[15] He suggested secularism could pattern itself after the biblical prophets' critiques of those who misrepresented God's will, pointing to how the prophets' negation of false religion was grounded in "the affirmation of the reality and power and holiness of God who is other than, greater than and more enduring than any human institution or achievement." Newbigin questioned, "If that affirmation [of God] be denied, can the secular spirit end otherwise than in a self-destructive nihilism?"[16]

He pressed this point, especially in terms of the psychological impact that jettisoning God would have on people. Relating the story of a friend who was a scientist working on the American nuclear program, Newbigin wrote,

Are we taking seriously into account the other side of the picture, the sense of meaninglessness and even of terror with which modern secularized man faces his future? Was my Chicago friend not typical of the best of modern man in his combination of rejoicing in the skills that could produce a controlled nuclear reaction, and his fore-boding at the sense that he and his colleagues were releasing a demon which was more likely to destroy mankind than to be the servant of mankind?[17]

Secularism not only left humans defenseless to deal with bogeymen of their own creation because they could not look beyond their own re-sources for help, but it also, ironically, turned people back to even faultier religious beliefs. He cited the rise of astrology in the Western world as an example of this and queried, "Is it quite certain that the ancient gods are buried beyond the possibility of haunting us again?"[18]

In sum, Newbigin believed secularism was a power for good that the church should recognize and embrace. The church should acknowledge that it had benefited from secularism eroding the apathy of Christendom that had made the Christian faith missionally impotent for centuries. It should also proudly claim that Christian missionaries worked in tandem with the secular efforts to improve people's standard of living and quality of life around the world. As Newbigin put it, "Missionaries in Asia and Africa have been agents of secularization even if they did not realize it. Like the first Christians who refused obeisance either to the pagan gods or to the divine Emperor."[19]

At the same time, Christians should not accept the logic of secularism on its face. They needed to imbue it with the affirmation of God's reality and, more than that, the message of the gospel. In doing this, they could transfigure secularism, moving it from being perceived as an enemy to religion to an act of God:

> Secularization . . . is the present revolutionary phase of the impact of the biblical message upon mankind. It is a process which puts

---

[17]Newbigin, *Honest Religion for Secular Man*, 34.
[18]Newbigin, *Honest Religion for Secular Man*, 34.
[19]Newbigin, *Honest Religion for Secular Man*, 18.

men in the situation of having to make new decisions, upon which depend the possibilities of freedom or bondage. The Christian Church in every land is called to the task of being witness to what God is doing in this worldwide process, so that those who are being drawn out of their traditional securities into this new and perplexing freedom may be helped to understand this experience as what it truly is, a calling to new responsibility before the Lord of history. . . . The task of the missionary . . . will be to be the interpreter who stands at the point where secularization is cutting into the ancient way of life, making clear by his word and his manner of life the way in which a Christian can accept the offer of freedom which secularization brings. . . . A truly biblical understanding of the process of secularization will lead the Church out to the frontiers where that process is most vigorously at work, to be the interpreter of the offer of freedom and of the threat of bondage which are hidden within the movement of secularization.[20]

In case his words were not sufficient, Newbigin concluded by citing the prayer Jesus offered on behalf of his disciples prior to his crucifixion:

My prayer is not that you take them out of the world but that you protect them from the evil one. They are not of the world, even as I am not of it. Sanctify them by the truth; your word is truth. As you sent me into the world, I have sent them into the world. For them I sanctify myself, that they too may be truly sanctified. (John 17:15-19)

Thus, for Newbigin Christians should be engaged with secularism by working alongside the secular agencies that seek to liberate people to choose better lives (he even cited the work of the UN approvingly[21]). In doing this, these agencies are agents of God's work. Christians are the interpreters who help both the secular agencies and those the agencies

---

[20]Newbigin, *Honest Religion for Secular Man*, 137.
[21]Newbigin, *Honest Religion for Secular Man*, 13.

are helping to recognize God's presence in their work, protecting all of them from falling into the abyss of nihilism.

Newbigin makes a compelling case. Christians can welcome secularism and secularists as joint workers to improve people's standard of living and quality of life. Indeed, there are ways that secular organizations might bring these aspects of abundant life more effectively than the church can on its own.

There is one point missing from Newbigin's argument, however. He does not contend with the fact that the church is not the only group seeking to fill the lacuna created by secularism having a negation without an affirmation. As Stone warned, various powers and principalities want to exploit the freedom secularism offers by luring people to choose a new life that is loyal to them. Secularism is not evil because of this, but it also does not offer any direction for how those it touches should arbitrate among the voices beckoning their allegiance. If the church is to be faithful to Christ's mission, it must not only be explicit about its understanding of abundant life as it works with secular organizations but also invite others to share that belief. Further, it should present it in a way that is winsome, creative, and gracious enough that makes it more attractive to people than other invitations for how they should believe and live.

E. Stanley Jones. E. Stanley Jones, a Methodist missionary to India and a contemporary of Newbigin's, recognized this. Encountering the same human struggles in India as in the United States, he wrote, "Human need and human sin are not geographical. Materialism, greed, moral failure and spiritual yearning are in the East and in the West."[22] His response to this was to emphasize the person of Jesus and to let go of the Western culture that missionaries often sought to push along with the gospel. He explained in *The Christ of India Road*:

When I first went to India, I was trying to hold a very long line—a line that stretched clear from Genesis to Revelation, on to Western

---

[22]E. Stanley Jones, *Christ at the Round Table* (New York: Abingdon, 1928), 4.

Civilization and to the Western Christian Church. I found myself
bobbing up and down that line fighting behind Moses and David
and Jesus and Paul and Western Civilization and the Christian
Church. I was worried. There was no well-defined issue. . . . I had
the ill-defined but distinctive feeling that the heart of the matter
was being left out. Then I saw that I could, and should, shorten my
line, that I could take my stand at Christ and . . . refuse to know
anything save Jesus Christ and him crucified. . . . I saw that the
gospel lies in the person of Jesus, that he himself is the Good News,
that my one task was to live and to present him.[23]

By letting go of Western civilization, Jones unencumbered himself from
the economic, political, social, and other powers that might seek to woo
people's hearts and minds as secularization did its work. Instead, he could
focus on the freeing message of the gospel of Jesus Christ, offering the
fullness of salvation without curtsying to the unjust systems that would
otherwise encompass his ministry.

This salvation required sharing the gospel so that people could become
disciples of Jesus Christ. It also entailed working for the betterment of
people's lives on earth. Jones was explicit about this:

He [Jesus] does not fit in with things as they are. He meets them
with "an abrupt challenge." It is this challenge that stabs our souls
and our civilizations awake. As long as little children toil in factories
under inhuman conditions, as long as those who have exploit those
who have not, as long as stronger nations suppress weaker ones, as
long as might is the arbiter among classes and nations, as long as
priest-craft exploits credulity and fattens upon it, as long as woman
is treated as a chattel and the tool of man's lust, as long as one of
these little ones is caused to stumble, as long as the Father is not
known and realized and the brotherhood of our humanity not a

---

[23]E. Stanley Jones, *The Christ of the Indian Road*, 6th ed. (Nashville: United Methodist Publishing
House, 1953), 11-12.

working fact, as long as the Kingdom has not come, and as long as men need to repent for anything, Jesus stands with his abrupt challenge. That challenge is our salvation.[24]

For Jones, this sort of work could involve joining forces with those who were of different religions or no religion. His reason for this was akin to Newbigin's. Any work that sought to do good was work that belonged to God. Therefore, the Christian had full liberty to participate along with anyone doing that work. He grounded this in the admonition Paul gave in 1 Corinthians 3:22: "The apostle sums up everything and cries, 'All things belong to you.' The liberty is complete. Nothing of reality is left out. Here is the great affirming of life. Here is salvation in its root idea of wholeness or health. Christ is life's complete affirmation."[25]

Like Newbigin, Jones found an affirmation to fill the hole in secularism. It was Jesus. What Jones insisted on was that it was Jesus *alone*. When Jesus was one of many agendas, human aspirations would creep in along with their vices and overtake the salvation being offered. When Jesus was the only agenda, Christians were set free to be disciples of Jesus Christ who could challenge the unjust powers of this world such that other people, especially those in need, could experience the fullness of life. Jesus was the backbone for Christians resisting and replacing the evils that might come about from an unchecked secularism. As the Lausanne Covenant would state later, "The salvation we claim should be transforming us in the totality of our personal and social responsibilities."[26]

Part of the way Jesus provides Christians this freedom is by letting them see themselves through the eyes of those they serve, just as Jones came to see himself through the eyes of the Indians. It was only after he realized that the Indians saw him as trying to defend Western civilization and church institutions that he was able to step away from that and center

---

[24]Jones, *Christ at the Round Table*, 106.
[25]Jones, *Christ at the Round Table*, 327.
[26]"The Lausanne Covenant," Lausanne Movement, section 5, www.lausanne.org/content/covenant/lausanne-covenant.

his life on Jesus alone. The ability to call people to become disciples of Jesus and to care for others' physical needs in partnership with secular agencies flowed from that center. Jesus was not forced to adapt to the secular goals of improving people's standard of living or quality of life. Neither did Jesus have to accept only specific practices of making disciples. Rather, Jesus provided both the motivation and template for all this work.

The distinctive for Christians, then, is not in their practice of helping others. We will feed the hungry, clothe the naked, care for the sick, befriend the lonely, and challenge the unjust leader in much the same way as a secular person of goodwill. The difference is that we follow the example, teachings, and salvific work of Jesus Christ in how we carry out this work.

With this focus on Jesus firmly in place, both Newbigin and Jones aver that Christians can participate in abundant life while working hand in hand with secular agencies. All who work for others to receive any portion of God's life are welcome partners. This can be done untainted by the evils that try to co-opt Christianity by keeping Jesus at the center of the work.[27] Moreover, by working for the common good with others, we can demonstrate that the Christian belief in eternity pulls Christians toward caring about this world and the people in it. We can share the full story of abundant life with them. This is better than the alternatives: letting go of the eternal because we do not want to appear too strange or offensive as we work toward improving people's lives in this world or refusing to be engaged with this world because we believe God cares only about eternity.

---

[27]Newbigin, Jones, and I (Mark) emphasize Jesus being at the center because of our Protestant leanings. It is important to recognize that other Christians, especially the Eastern Orthodox churches, would want to supplement this talk of Jesus with a fuller reference to the Trinity. The nature of the Trinity is itself one of missional sharing and stewardship among the three persons (Father, Son, and Holy Spirit), and the call to *theosis* (or divinization) is in part a call to enter into that divine life of charity and generosity toward others. The wide variety of saints the church honors points to the various ways they can demonstrate this holy life by caring for people's standard of living and quality of life even as they serve as witnesses to the eternal glory of the triune God.

A CHALLENGE TO PARTISANS ON THE THEOLOGICAL SPECTRUM AND RE-IMAGINING MISSIONS

The narrative of John 3:16 is important, powerful, and essential to the Christian faith: God loves us and sends Jesus to provide us eternal life in place of death. It is a message worth proclaiming far and wide. Still, it is not the entire narrative of the Christian faith. God does not just want us to experience eternal life in glory. God wants us to experience life now. There is no break between the "here and now" and the "hereafter"; there is just one unbroken abundant life God offers us to enjoy.

The eternal facet of abundant life does mean that we have a unique motivation for how we live as Christians. We are preparing ourselves for judgment. We will be judged on whether we have responded in faith to God's offer of abundant life through Jesus, both by whether we have believed in the work of Jesus and whether we have loved God and our neighbors. We show this love through tangible activities: recognizing God as the source of all good gifts in this world and the next, receiving these gifts, and being faithful stewards of all we have received. This stewardship includes improving the standard of living and quality of life of those in need as well as proclaiming the forgiveness of sins and the promise of eternal life through Christ.

This way of participating in abundant life stands as a challenge to those who defend reduced views of salvation. Conservatives who want to claim that salvation is only about what happens after death are challenged to realize that, while it is necessary to accept the forgiveness of God and profess faith in Jesus Christ, it is just as necessary to improve people's standard of living and quality of life in this world. Doing both is required to be judged favorably by God. Liberals who want to claim that salvation and damnation are simply constructs related to human experiences of happiness and misery, and so focus only on improving people's standard of living and quality of life, are challenged to realize that without the crucified and risen Jesus even their most prophetic stances will ultimately fall victim to the agendas of the principalities and powers they deplore.

The call for both these groups is the same: stretch your thinking. The point is not to lift one aspect of abundant life over another. It is for the church to recognize that salvation is multifaceted, taking place across time and space. The result is that the church should order itself, and individual Christians should commit themselves, to work toward inviting people into the fullness of salvation, which is the abundant life Jesus offers. The only alternative to this, as Alan Hirsch and Mark Nelson describe, is a "hellish existence" in which "we experience a reduced life, which in turn implies that we settle for all sorts of substitutes. And when the substitutes become the norm, we find ourselves living very comfortably, embracing the art of settling."[28]

The debates about whether humanitarian aid or evangelism is more important miss the point. The point is that the Bible portrays salvation as creation being rescued from chaos and darkness to live into the fullest blessings of God in the present and the future. Anything that works toward this rescue and establishing people in this life is a faithful act in God's purpose. And, on the day of judgment, when God asks if we fed the hungry, clothed the naked, befriended the sick and imprisoned, shared the gospel, baptized new Christians, and made disciples—thus sharing all the aspects of abundant life with others—God will not care what theology we held when we did those things or whether we worked with people from secular organizations or if we used secular terminology to help us explain what we were doing. God will simply care that we did them and will say to those of us who have, "Well done, good and faithful servant! You have been faithful with a few things; I will put you in charge of many things. Come and share your master's happiness!" (Matthew 25:21).

And that will mean we will continue participating in abundant life eternally.

---

[28]Hirsch and Nelson, *Reframation*, 88.

7

Salvation Today

Weeping may stay for the night,
but rejoicing comes in the morning.

PSALM 30:5

THE PSALMIST SPEAKS the hope of humanity. Weeping is all too common for us. We recognize that we live in a time that is bound by chaos and darkness. Just as the ancients longed for a hero that could bind the cosmic forces that generated suffering, misery and death, we are no less desperate to find an escape. The standard of living and the quality of life for vast swaths of the earth's population are abysmally low. People die from lacking the ability to consume the necessities of life, and they battle the multiple destructive effects that come from loneliness, isolation, and stress. The problems leading to this situation are remarkably complex and defy human effort to overcome them. We saw the exacerbation of all of this in the Covid-19 pandemic and the glaring spotlight put on institutional racism.

As if this was not enough, we have the existential threat of death looming over us. Like Hamlet wondering whether we "dream" when we fall asleep in death, we struggle with an uncertainty that we simply cannot pierce. What happens to us when we die? Will we simply cease to exist, or will there be a judgment of some sort, calling us to account for how we have lived and what we have believed?

What we yearn for is salvation. Salvation that unsnarls the chaotic forces destroying life in this world and that shines light on the deep darkness of the grave with the assurance that something good waits for us. We need a salvation that is both earthy and heavenly, one that meets us in the muck of our physical, psychological, political, economic, and social needs and that inspires us spiritually. We need life that is abundant, unmarred by pain and death.

Since we are not the ancient writers, we also need a way to talk about this salvation that is not premised on mythological genres. We need language and concepts that will make sense in a post-Enlightenment, secular culture. We need ways to measure this salvation that will show we are attaining it as individuals and communities of faith as well as sharing it with everyone in need locally and internationally.

By making use of the terms *standard of living* and *quality of life*, we have that language and measurement. We can recast the Christian experience of salvation using secular vocabulary and metrics, giving the secular world a way of understanding salvation that it has not had before. By linking them to *eternal life*, we ground these ideas in our Christian hope for glory.

These terms are not just helpful for communicating the Christian experience of salvation to those who are outside the church. By deploying these terms, those of us in the church are given new tools for rediscovering what we believe about salvation. We have become so influenced by secular thinking, formed by our regional and socioeconomic situations, and so hardened in our partisan theological traditions that many of us can scarcely articulate what salvation entails anymore. We are called to reflect on what we understand salvation to be and recognize the paucity of it.

By seriously considering these terms, we are driven back into the whole Bible, finding that God has a much larger vision of salvation for us than most of the common ways Christians describe it. It is cosmic in scope, caring both for our daily needs in this world as well as for our eternal state. It saves us from physical privation as well as our own pettiness and sin, giving us all we need for our bodies, our minds, and our spirits now and eternally. In short, it offers us abundant life through Jesus Christ. More than that, it invites us to participate in abundant life.

The concepts of standard of living, quality of life, and eternal life offer

- A way to start conversations about working for the common good between Christians and secular people.

- A foundation for those who are secular to consider how people of faith can do good in the world through practicing their religion.

- A reason for all people to start partnering with others of goodwill to strive for the common good.

- A way for Christians to start working across theological, regional, racial, and socioeconomic divides within the church to accomplish the good that all Christians believe God wants others to share, especially those who are neediest.

- Ways to start bridging the divide between practices of ministry we long thought to be antithetical, such as evangelism, humanitarian aid, and community organizing.

- Inspiration to start stewarding the good things that we have been given, including our finances, our belongings, our time, and the gospel message.

- A tangible reason to start exploring the eternal promises of Jesus because we can see how the kingdom of God is made manifest now.

- A warning that we must give an account before God at the final judgment based on not just what we believe but how we have lived.

- A way to measure ministry effectiveness that is both meaningful to the Christian faith and to those outside the church.

In all this, they point to practical, empirically verifiable ways that we can both live into salvation and offer salvation to others. And, in doing that, they offer us hope that salvation is not something that is far in the future but rather something that has the power to inspire and unite people now. A vision of abundant life that syncs with what everyone understands is the common good, even if we start with just the parts of life that relate to the physical world, is powerful.

Many Christian organizations and congregations are already doing some of these things. This is excellent. The challenge for these groups is the same challenge I put before the students in my evangelism course: to articulate why they are doing them. How are they grounded in and informed by the gospel message? How do they demonstrate the Christian experience of salvation, not just a secular humanitarianism? How are both the Christians who are helping and the people they seek to help given the opportunity to receive and participate in the abundant life of God?

An Ancient Path

The idea of abundant life linking together our physical and eternal well-being has long been part of the church's thinking. The Divine Liturgy of St. John Chrysostom, which has existed since the fourth century and continues to be used today in Eastern Orthodox churches, is witness to this.

Throughout the liturgy, a series of petitions is offered to God in prayer. Each grouping of these petitions is called an *ectenia*. The focus of these petitions is on salvation; however, that salvation takes many forms. In the Great Ectenia, which is the set of petitions at the beginning of the liturgy, we find multiple references to standard of living (physical needs), quality of life (psychological well-being and community), and eternal life (forgiveness of sin and life after death). These petitions are both for the people who are praying and for others. They lift up especially those who are suffering or who face potential danger, even desiring peace and salvation for the world and ecological well-being in the form of seasonal weather and good crops.

Deacon: In peace let us pray to the Lord.

Choir: Lord, have mercy.

Deacon: For the peace from above, and the salvation of our souls, let us pray to the Lord.

Choir: Lord, have mercy.

Deacon: For the peace of the whole world, the good estate of the holy churches of God, and the union of all, let us pray to the Lord.

Choir: Lord, have mercy.

Deacon: For this holy temple, and for them that with faith, reverence, and the fear of God enter herein, let us pray to the Lord.

Choir: Lord, have mercy.

Deacon: For the Orthodox episcopate [include names of various hierarchs]; for the venerable priesthood, the diaconate in Christ, for all the clergy and people, let us pray to the Lord.

Choir: Lord, have mercy.

Deacon: For the suffering Orthodox people both in the homeland and in the diaspora, and for their salvation, let us pray to the Lord.

Choir: Lord, have mercy.

Deacon: For this land, its authorities and armed forces, let us pray to the Lord.

Choir: Lord, have mercy.

Deacon: That He may deliver His people from enemies visible and invisible and confirm in us oneness of mind, brotherly love, and piety, let us pray to the Lord.

Choir: Lord, have mercy.

Deacon: For this city, for every city and country, and the faithful that dwell therein, let us pray to the Lord.

Choir: Lord, have mercy.

Deacon: For seasonable weather, abundance of the fruits of the earth, and peaceful times, let us pray to the Lord.

Choir: Lord, have mercy.

Deacon: For travelers by sea, land, and air; for the sick, the suffering, the imprisoned, and for their salvation, let us pray to the Lord.

Choir: Lord, have mercy.

Deacon: That we may be delivered from all tribulation, wrath, and necessity, let us pray to the Lord.

Choir: Lord, have mercy.

Deacon: Help us, save, have mercy on us, and keep us, O God, by Thy grace.

Choir: Lord, have mercy.[1]

Later in the service, as the people prepare for Holy Communion, the deacon prays the Ectenia of Fervent Supplication. He repeats some of the petitions above, then adds the following petitions that focus on quality of life (a clear conscience, a sense of peace, an escape from pain) and eternal life (forgiveness of sins, preparation for death, and a good final judgment):

Deacon: That the whole day may be perfect, holy, peaceful, and sinless, let us ask of the Lord.

Choir: Grant this, O Lord.

Deacon: An angel of peace, a faithful guide, a guardian of our souls and bodies, let us ask of the Lord.

Choir: Grant this, O Lord.

Deacon: Pardon and remission of our sins and offenses, let us ask of the Lord.

Choir: Grant this, O Lord.

---

[1] *Prayer Book*, rev. 4th ed. (Jordanville, NY: Printshop of Saint Job of Pochaev, 1996), 97-100.

Deacon: Things good and profitable for our souls, and peace for the world, let us ask of the Lord.

Choir: Grant this, O Lord.

Deacon: That we may complete the remaining time of our life in peace and repentance, let us ask of the Lord.

Choir: Grant this, O Lord.

Deacon: A Christian ending to our life, painless, blameless, peaceful, and a good defense before the dread judgment seat of Christ, let us ask of the Lord.

Choir: Grant this, O Lord.[2]

Finally, as the congregation awaits Holy Communion, the choir draws on an even deeper repository of faith to explain the fullness of salvation that awaits the faithful by reciting Psalm 23 (KJV as quoted below). The opening two verses speak to the high standard of living God offers:

The LORD is my shepherd; I shall not want.

He maketh me to lie down in green pastures: he leadeth me beside the still waters.

The next three verses speak to how God provides a high quality of life, guiding people to live in a good way, assuring them in the face of evil and death, comforting and providing for them when struggling with those who would harm them:

He restoreth my soul: he leadeth me in the paths of righteousness for his name's sake.

Yea, though I walk through the valley of the shadow of death, I will fear no evil: for thou art with me; thy rod and thy staff they comfort me.

Thou preparest a table before me in the presence of mine enemies: thou anointest my head with oil; my cup runneth over.

---

[2]*Prayer Book*, 123-25.

The final verse pivots from this world to the next, recognizing the forgiveness of sins and eternal life that flows from God:

> Surely goodness and mercy shall follow me all the days of my life:
> and I will dwell in the house of the LORD for ever.

The culmination of this is receiving Holy Communion. This act embodies the fullness of the abundant life of Christ for the Orthodox. In it we are sustained physically through a meal (standard of living), we are encouraged by the community of believers around us (quality of life), and we share in the "fountain of immortality," a term the choir chants while the congregation communes (eternal life).

While these prayers have been modified over time (the reference to air travel, for instance, was not in the fourth-century text), the core petitions have stood as part of the Divine Liturgy for over a millennium. They are witnesses to how the church has long intertwined standard of living, quality of life, and eternal life as composing the abundant life that Jesus offers us. Christians, like all humans, want to enjoy a good standard of living and quality of life while they live, and they want to have assurance of eternal life when they die. Christians have always believed that Jesus offers all of this, and Christians have always prayed for God to share all these gifts of life with the whole world.

Using the words that are common to secular institutions today simply gives us new ways to describe and understand these prayers. It doesn't change how these prayers cry out to God for salvation by asking for every aspect of abundant life for ourselves and others.

THE RIGHT TIME

The pastor cited in the introduction who wrote for help training his congregation in articulating the Christian faith was asking a bigger question than he may have realized. Answering it requires learning not just the vocabulary of salvation but a new way of conceptualizing how Christians live in the world.

Rather than just talk about a salvation that will be completed once-for-all in the future (e.g., the hope of heaven, justice in this world, or generically getting saved), we can talk about experiencing salvation in an ongoing way that begins now and stretches unbroken into eternity. We have this experience because God offers us abundant life, which both blesses us and calls us to share that life with others. As we receive and share, we participate in abundant life.

This participation changes the logic of how Christians engage with each other and with the world. It opens the door for us to take seriously the experiences of Christians around the world, especially those who come from the Majority World, and to recognize that their theology should share equally in shaping our theological traditions. It also provides a platform for us to engage with secular contexts more effectively, giving us a firm soteriological foundation for working alongside people of goodwill who seek to improve the lives of others while also providing us language and metrics to explain our faith in Jesus to those outside the church in a way they can understand better.

Central to all of this is that the core concepts are attended by verbs. We do not just think about Christian salvation; we *experience* salvation. We *receive* and *share* salvation in an ongoing way. In doing this, we *participate* in abundant life. This way of understanding abundant life requires us to do more than just articulate our message; we must embody our message in how we speak, act, and move through our daily lives. In more conventional language, it is a call to be intentional in our Christian discipleship, learning that to be unapologetically Christian in the public square is more compelling than being either (1) unapologetically Christian as a separated people who judge others or (2) apologetically Christian in public by downplaying the full Christian story of salvation.

In doing this, local congregations can move, as evangelism professor W. Jay Moon explains it, from "making ice blocks to making ice cubes."[3]

---

[3] W. Jay Moon, "Catching Water in the New Ecosystem," (address, annual meeting of the Great Commission Research Network, Asbury Theological Seminary, June 11, 2021).

Instead of trying to create an ever-larger footprint for the church as an institution, it can focus more on forming individual Christians as participants in abundant life. These Christians will then share that life in their respective spheres as they pray for, volunteer with, work alongside, and relate to the people they know. This more decentralized approach to the Christian witness will be far more effective. Just as one big block of ice can chill only one tub of water but lots of ice cubes can chill far more water by being distributed through dozens of glasses, so many scattered Christians will bring the cooling touch of God's healing to many more people caught in the fever of chaos, sin, darkness, and death.

The twenty-first century offers an excellent time for us to participate in abundant life. This is because everything is at a crossroads in the culture right now. As Andy Crouch explained regarding the Covid-19 pandemic, initially we thought we were just hunkering down for a blizzard that would affect us for a few weeks; then we thought we were in for a long winter that would last months; and now we realize that the impacts on our culture will be more like a mini–ice age because some things will never go back to the way they were.[4] Glaciers have shifted, avalanches have crashed down, and the topography has changed. The only option left for congregations is to consider themselves as new startups that depend "far more on radical innovation."[5]

While the pandemic may have forced this realization on many Christian congregations, the cultural landscape had long been demanding that congregations change. The statistics in the United States (and much of Europe) point to a decreasing number of people choosing to align themselves with Christianity. The reality of this is being felt in how many congregations are being forced to close their doors or cut back to survive. (I saw this firsthand one week when I visited one congregation that was announcing a reduction in staff and another that was selling off

---

[4]Andy Crouch, Kurt Keilhacker, and David Blanchard, "Leading Beyond the Blizzard: Why Every Organization Is Now a Startup," *The Praxis Journal*, March 20, 2020, https://journal.praxislabs.org /leading-beyond-the-blizzard-why-every-organization-is-now-a-startup-b7f32fb278ff.

[5]Crouch, Keilhacker, and Blanchard, "Leading Beyond the Blizzard."

substantial property, both because of declining attendance and budgets.) For those of us who have given most of our lives to the institutional church in some way, this is grim. We feel like we are on a losing team that is progressively less relevant to the world around us. The language in our hymns and liturgies that we so cherish seems archaic, the lyrics of our praise songs seem too detached from daily life, our patterns of life to-gether seem strange and out-of-touch, and even our own children don't see the wonder of the church the way we did at their age. We seem to be irrelevant, easily overlooked, and soon to be forgotten altogether.

Yet this is the thinking of those who make ice blocks. It is also the thinking of those who have forgotten that we are participating in the abundant life of God even now. When our congregations shift into the business of making ice cubes by forming each Christian to recognize the abundant life God has already given us and then equipping them to share that life, it changes our entire point of view. Suddenly, the size or shape of a congregation—or even a denomination—is not so critical. What matters is the cosmic-sized salvation we are living in now. It encompasses us individually, it encompasses our Christian communities (whatever form they take), and it encompasses the people with whom we share it (even if they do not realize it yet!). Living in this victory, we have no need to despair, just the call to participate in the life God is already pouring forth.

And, lest we forget, the church is not alone in having to reconsider how it forms itself. The entire Western culture is dealing with the ice-age ef-fects of the social unrest, distrust, and anger stemming from centuries of secularism that failed to find a core affirmation for people to share. This has allowed systemic injustices to go unchecked and deep divisions to form between peoples. It is not that the church is facing a shift and the culture is not, but that both are facing massive changes. The difference is that the church knows it can participate in God's abundant life in the midst of all this chaos.

It is the right time for participating in abundant life as a way of living out our salvation and sharing it with others. See! See there the coffins of those who have been touched by the death-dealing chaos in the world. The ones in them are not yet dead but are nearly so! There are the vast throngs of the poor, needy, displaced, hungry, thirsty, naked, and sick who are being carried out, desperate for someone to improve their standard of living. There are numberless lonely, forgotten, isolated, stressed, and rejected people who need someone to improve their quality of life. There is the entire population of the earth that faces its mortality and desires earnestly for eternal life that conquers death. Some people of goodwill are already at work among these masses, offering what they can. Today, as those who participate in abundant life, we can enter the mix in word and deed, and we can say alike to those who help and those who need help, "Live."

Appendix

Metrics for Salvation

At the LORD's command through Moses, each was
assigned his work and told what to carry. Thus they
were counted, as the LORD commanded Moses.

NUMBERS 4:49

STATISTICAL REPORTS HAVE LONG BEEN part of church life. These reports track how many people congregations are reaching and what sorts of resources and activities congregations have available. However, these reports can seem lifeless compared to the transformative power of salvation. As Gil Rendle, author of *Doing the Math of Mission*, wrote in his introduction, "Can, in fact, ministry be measured in mathematical proportions?"[1] Numbers would seem inadequate for this task, forcing us to reduce our ministry to statistics and causing us to miss the most important data: stories of transformation.

Given the multifaceted nature of salvation, the church can take a cue from Moses in the passage above. The book of Numbers, as indicated by its title, relates a detailed census that God commanded Moses to take of

---

[1] Gil Rendle, *Doing the Math of Mission: Fruits, Faithfulness, and Metrics* (New York: Rowman & Littlefield, 2014), 1.

the Israelites. The census was not just to determine the entire number of Israelites but to determine the specific numbers of people from each tribe who could serve God in different ways. Some were to serve in the army, some as priests, some as helpers in the tabernacle, and some in other ways. The counting was not to homogenize the people but to differentiate them by their gifts and to recognize the variety of ways they could serve God.

This appendix will look at some practical ways to quantify the effectiveness of congregations as they participate in abundant life, including how they address the standard of living, quality of life, and eternal life of those both inside and outside the congregation.

Given the wide variety of ways that participation in abundant life could be measured, the ideas presented here are meant to be suggestive rather than absolute. Each congregation will need to think about the ways it participates in abundant life and consider how to quantify those. The score cards especially are not meant to lay down specifics that must be measured but rather to encourage congregations to consider how they can hold themselves accountable for participating in every aspect of abundant life in concrete and actionable ways.

THE MATH OF MISSION

Before getting to the actual metrics, we should start with a quick overview of the logic behind metrics. It is not just a matter of collecting numbers. Rather, it is about gathering information that tells the story of how an organization is carrying out its mission. In the case of congregations, the question is whether they are effectively participating in abundant life.

Rendle offers two helpful insights about how metrics should be developed. First, he describes the process of bringing about transformation. Then he explains the difference between counting and measuring.

Drawing from the teachings of the engineer W. Edwards Deming, Rendle suggests there are three stages in the process leading to transformation: input, throughput, output/outcome. Inputs are the resources needed to bring about transformation. Throughputs are the activities that use the resources to cause transformation. Outputs/outcomes are the resulting transformation, showing whether the throughputs successfully used the inputs. Counting is used to ascertain the number of resources used as inputs and the number of activities used as throughputs. Measuring is used to describe the resulting transformation in the outputs/outcomes.[2]

While Rendle combines outputs and outcomes, other forms of evaluation break these out and add a final element called "impact." When using this expanded assessment model, the outputs are the immediate effect of the throughput activities on the input resources, the outcomes are the effects the outputs have when they are released into a larger context, and the impact is the long-term, aggregate effect the entire process has on larger systems.[3]

A simple example of this is making peanut butter and jelly sandwiches (see form A.1 for an example of how to report this data). The bread, peanut butter, jelly, utensils used to spread the ingredients, and the people needed to make the sandwiches would all be inputs. The activities of instructing the people how to make the sandwiches and the actual assembling of the sandwiches would be the throughputs. According to Rendle, the primary difference in deciding whether an item goes into the input or the throughput category has to do with whether the focus is on the noun or the verb.[4] The ingredients, tools, and volunteers are nouns and so are inputs. The instructing and the assembling are verbs and so are the throughputs. Inputs are best measured in the number of resources available to be transformed. Throughputs are best measured in terms of the number of activities undertaken and the amount of time each activity took to accomplish.[5]

---

[2]Rendle, *Doing the Math of Mission*, 13-16.
[3]Peter York, *A Funder's Guide to Evaluation: Leveraging Evaluation to Improve Nonprofit Effectiveness* (St. Paul, MN: Fieldstone Alliance, 2005), 10-13.
[4]Rendle, *Doing the Math of Mission*, 14-15.
[5]Rendle, *Doing the Math of Mission*, 23-24.

Ministry Metrics Report

INPUTS

Jars of peanut butter	20
Jars of jelly	20
Loaves of bread	30
Volunteers	5
Knives for ingredients	10

THROUGHPUTS

Opportunities for assembling the sandwiches	1
Time instructing people on how to assemble sandwiches	15 minutes
Time spent assembling the sandwiches	2 Hours

OUTPUTS

	Before Event	After Event
Number of assembled sandwiches	0	250

OUTCOMES

	Before Event	After Event
Number of people fed	0	200
Volunteer confidence in kitchen skill	5 out of 10	7 out of 10
Volunteer awareness of malnutrition in area	3 out of 10	9 out of 10

Impact

OUR VISION—To decrease malnutrition in our area, especially among children.

	Before Ministry	Three Years After Ministry Started
Children in area with access to free or reduced lunch during the summer	30 Percent	80 Percent

Form A.1. PBJ example for reporting ministry metrics

The outputs would be the sandwiches, which are the transformed inputs. The outcomes, which are an extension of the outputs, would be the transformation brought about by the sandwiches on people. In this case, since sandwiches are not meant to exist in perpetuity but to be eaten, one outcome would be how many people were fed by the sandwiches. Likewise, the volunteers making the sandwiches might be transformed in their kitchen skills, so their improved sandwich-making ability would be another outcome. The impact, which is a long-term effect of the entire process, might be a growing awareness of hunger in the area with a resulting concerted effort to decrease hunger through improved structures to provide affordable food to children in need.

Per Rendle, the inputs and throughputs are counted since they are easily quantified. The outputs, outcomes, and impact are measured because they deal with transformation. That said, this measurement can also be quantified. To do this, we must be careful to quantify them in a way that tracks change. This requires gathering information both before and after the throughput activities take place.

For example, an output would be that where there were no peanut butter and jelly sandwiches before the activity, there are now 250. An outcome would be that where no one was fed before the sandwiches were assembled, two hundred people were fed with those sandwiches. Another outcome would be that, while those making the sandwiches felt only somewhat confident making sandwiches before their participation, many of those people felt more confident after participating. An impact would be that while only 30 percent of children in the area had access to free or reduced lunches over the summer, now 80 percent do. All of these are ways of measuring the transformation through quantitative data taken before and after the activity.

This before-and-after structure for gathering data requires forethought. When preparing to engage in an activity, you must identify the transformation you want to occur. Then, establish a data point (something specific you can measure that you expect to change as a result of your activity) and make certain to measure it before and after your activity. In our example of the sandwiches, the organizers asked the volunteers to rate how confident they were in the kitchen both before and after the event, giving them a way to show transformation as a result of the activity.

Depending on how deep a dive you want to make into the data and where you want to measure the level of transformation your ministry is causing, you can set up multiple data points. For example, if the organizers of the sandwich-making activity hoped to inspire the volunteers to address pervasive hunger in the neighborhood, at the beginning of the event they could have asked the volunteers, "On a scale from one to ten, with one being the least and ten being the most, how severe do you think child malnutrition is in our neighborhood?" During the instruction time, the organizers would explain the scope of child malnutrition in that region along with demonstrating how to make the sandwiches. Then, when the event was over, they would ask their question again. This would measure whether being exposed to that information along with the activity made the participants more aware of local child hunger on a more systemic level. The key is being clear about the transformation you want to accomplish and then developing ways to gather data both before and after the activity to see whether that transformation has taken place.[6]

Impacts require both forethought and vision. You need to dream big about the ultimate effect you want your ministry to have. In our example, the vision was to decrease childhood hunger in the area. Again, there needs to be data points to determine if the ministry is making this sort of difference. The organizers in our example chose the accessibility of free and reduced lunches for children over the summer as their data point to measure this. This is not the only data point they could have used to

---

[6]Rendle, *Doing the Math of Mission*, 26-30.

measure if they were having a systemic impact on child malnutrition in the area, but it is the way they thought was most appropriate for their context.

Since the impact offers a picture of what you ultimately hope to accomplish, even though it is the last step in the process, it is best to start by articulating the impact. Cast your vision, then start building a process that will lead you to it. It takes several steps, but each can help build on the other. In our example, the volunteers make sandwiches to feed the hungry; while doing this, the volunteers become more proficient in the kitchen and more aware of childhood hunger in their area. The benefit of increased kitchen proficiency and awareness of childhood hunger causes them to become more committed to making the sandwiches and likely prompts them to invite more people to help with the work in the future. As more volunteers are brought in, the capacity for making more sandwiches and feeding more people expands. So does the capacity for promoting political change. Over time (it could take weeks, months, or years), the aggregate of all this allows for the organizers of the sandwich activity to assert the needed political pressure to have the city council make free or reduced lunches available to children over the summer. From simple sandwich making to systemic transformation via the transformation of individuals along the way!

One other point worth recognizing about the outputs, outcomes, and impacts is that they all look beyond the institution that births them. Congregations are often tempted to measure only the things they can use to build their size and effectiveness (these are usually the inputs, such as the number of people who attend worship or the amount of money given through the offering). This is easy to count. The problem is, this does not take into account that—like the sandwiches—congregations are not meant to exist only for themselves. They are meant to be in mission to others. So, they need to measure what effect they are having outside their walls. We will address this in more detail later below.

SECULAR METRICS

As mentioned earlier in the book, one of the benefits of using the concepts of standard of living and quality of life is that they have established metrics connected to them. These metrics were developed by secular humanitarian agencies. Notwithstanding, they are thoughtful and helpful. Using them will allow Christians to demonstrate that they are working for the common good in a secular context. We can learn three broad lessons from these metrics that deal with bringing life: they (1) must be large, (2) will likely be complex, and (3) must be revisable.

Large metrics: Targets and goals. As we have already seen, secular agencies that improve people's standard of living have tools to measure if their work is effective. The Human Development Index (HDI), which looks at income and consumption or the immediate impact of these on a population (such as longer lifespans or greater access to education), is an example of this.

Tools like this are enormous, requiring a vast amount of data to be collected, integrated, and interpreted. The HDI relies on census data about lifespan, statistics from primary and secondary schools and schools of higher education, and the computation of the GDP. All of these are gathered and run through a mathematical formula to determine a single score that quantifies standard of living.

Congregations are dealing with something that is also very large when considering how to quantify whether they are participating in abundant life. They are measuring their impact as agents of God's transformative work in the world. This will likely involve combining several smaller measurements into one larger measurement. In assessment terminology, this is sometimes referred to as establishing targets (smaller measurements) that all contribute to showing if an overall outcome or goal (the larger measurement) is accomplished. For example, by measuring the targets of lifespan, education, and gross national income per capita, the UN can calculate the overall measurement of standard of living with the HDI score.

Harkening to Rendle, the language of targets and goals reminds us that these measurements are linked to the impact we want to make. They also serve as internal accountability checks on whether we are living toward that impact. In the case of the UN, the HDI, along with the targets that constitute it, relates to specific ways it seeks to improve people's standard of living.

Applying this, a congregation might set a goal of having a positive impact on those who are poor in its neighborhood. It could choose to measure this with the output of whether it improves the standard of living for one hundred people a year. To measure whether it is doing this, it could set targets of helping at least fifty people through a food pantry, twenty people with rental or utilities assistance, twenty people with gas cards, and ten people with emergency lodgings. By setting the specific targets, it could measure clearly whether it fulfilled its overall goal, which is much larger and much harder to quantify on its own. It also could determine what resources and activities (inputs and throughputs) were most needed to fulfill this goal.

Complex metrics. Metrics needed to measure whether a congregation is participating in abundant life are not only large but complex. This is shown by the need for multiple targets to feed into each goal because the goals are often too broad to be measured when they stand alone.

With complexity comes differing opinions about which measurements are needed to determine whether a goal is being met. For example, as we saw in chapter four, Paul Collier critiques the standard of living measurements that humanitarian aid agencies use to show the effectiveness of their work. He argues that they do not reflect the increasingly dire plight of the poorest nations that cannot access the wealth made available through globalization.

Even when there is agreement on how to measure something, the complexity of what is being measured can make it difficult to settle on which metrics to use. We saw this in relation to quality of life measurements. While researchers have isolated variables that seem to improve people's happiness, such as friendship or being part of a community, that experience of happiness is still subjective. The OECD's Better Life Index acknowledges this by allowing individuals to weight the variables that compose it so they can create their personalized basket of components that would make them happiest.

If there is this sort of disagreement and complexity among agencies that employ numerous experts to advise them on how best to measure the goals of improving people's lives in this world, it is little wonder that congregations or even denominations would experience the same thing. Such uncertainty and disagreement are even more likely because the church seeks to transform people's lives in the physical world and into eternity.

This suggests that a congregation should plan on putting significant time and energy into discussing what they believe salvation is, what aspects they feel most equipped to offer, and what specific problems they feel most called to address. Using a tool like the evangelism equation to guide this discussion would be a significant aid.[7] It helps them to talk about salvation in a way that is authentic to their personal experiences, true to the Christian faith, and meaningful to those who are to receive salvation. From this, they could develop a set of creative goals with targets that would guide their practices and give them something to measure. These conversations should not happen only once. They need to be ongoing.

Able to be revised. While the abundant life God offers is timeless, always seeking to improve people's standard of living and quality of life and inviting people to be forgiven and received into eternal life as a disciple of Jesus Christ, no measurement tool is perfect or should remain unchanged over time. Especially as new research and understanding become available, it is important to shift tools to fit with the new styles of ministry that a congregation will be developing.

---

[7]Mark R. Teasdale, *Evangelism for Non-Evangelists: Sharing the Faith Authentically* (Downers Grove, IL: InterVarsity Press, 2016).

This kind of revision is common among secular agencies. The HDI, for example, has changed over the years as new ways of calculating people's standard of living were developed. It was most recently updated in 2010. The Better Life Index did not even exist until 2011, when the need to measure well-being beyond consumption and income became clear. Even after being established, it has been consistently revised to account for newer studies that better reflect what makes people happy.

Not only do the measurement tools need to be reviewed and potentially modified regularly; so do the goals and targets underlying those measurements. As these change the measurements need to change with them.

One of the most wide-ranging shifts in goals among secular agencies took place when the United Nations moved from the Millennium Development Goals (MDGs) to the Sustainable Development Goals (SDGs). The MDGs were established by the UN in 2000 with the plan to achieve them by 2015. The SDGs were put in place in 2016 to improve on the work that had begun under the MDGs.

While the SDGs were a continuation of the MDGs, they also differed from them in two broad ways. First, they expanded the number of goals from eight to seventeen. Many of the new goals involved promoting what had been targets within larger goals of the MDGs to become goals in their own right. This was especially the case for goals dealing with ways to care for the environment that had previously all fallen under a single MDG. The reason for this was the new information that had come to light about the state of the environment between 2000 and 2015.

Second, the SDGs refined the targets that would have to be reached for each goal to be achieved. This refining took into account that much had already been accomplished to improve people's standard of living during the previous fifteen years, the growing concern that poorer countries were not seen as equal participants in enacting these goals, and the realization that the goals often overlapped. By considering all of this, the UN was able to develop new targets that continued the core work of improving people's standard of living in a way that also increased the agency of the people receiving most of the aid. It also found ways to work toward multiple goals by having shared targets that supported them.

For example, the first MDG was to eradicate extreme poverty. The first target toward accomplishing this goal was to reduce by half the number of people who lived on less than $1 (later revised to $1.25) per day. By 2015, this target had been partially achieved, with the number of people in developing regions of the world living in extreme poverty dropping from 47 percent to 22 percent of the global population, and the number of people worldwide living in extreme poverty dropping by a total of 700 million.[8]

Given the excellent outcome it helped drive, the first MDG was a solid goal, and its first target was useful. Still, the UN felt it could be improved. As a result, when developing the SDGs, the UN kept the same goal but developed more nuanced targets for it. The first target for the updated goal gives us a good sense for how they did this:

> By 2030, reduce at least by half the proportion of men, women and children of all ages living in poverty in all its dimensions according to national definitions. Implement nationally appropriate social protection systems . . . and by 2030 achieve substantial coverage of the poor and the vulnerable.[9]

While still working toward the same goal, this target strikes a different tone than the MDG target. It contextualizes what poverty looks like based on a nation's standard of living, calling on local governments to care for those living below the poverty line rather than assuming the UN alone will provide the needed aid. It also recognizes the interrelatedness of this goal and other SDGs. Another SDG is to create equality for men and women. By calling on nations in this target of the first SDG to care

---

[8]UN Department of Public Information, *Millennium Development Goals and Beyond 2015 Fact Sheet*, September 2013, www.un.org/millenniumgoals/pdf/Goal_1_fs.pdf.
[9]"Goal 1: End Poverty in All Its Forms Everywhere," Sustainable Development Goals, United Nations, www.un.org/sustainabledevelopment/poverty/.

equally for men, women, and children, it points to how eradicating poverty also involves overcoming economically entrenched forms of sexism.

There are extensive disagreements over the merits of the actual goals and the effectiveness of the shift from the MDGs to the SDGs. For our purposes, it is enough to recognize that even an agency like the UN with large, established goals that everyone can agree are good in the broadest sense, such as ending poverty, still needs to review its goals and the metrics it uses to determine if it is attaining them.

Congregations likewise have a large goal of participating in abundant life. This does not change, but the context, tools, and emphases of how we share that life will change over time. Like the UN, we should plan on setting aside regular times of conversation to review what God has called us to do and consider if we are doing it as effectively as we can. We should also review if the tools we are using to measure our effectiveness are as helpful as they could be in guiding us to accomplish our salvific goals.

With these lessons in place to guide us in establishing, reviewing, and revising our goals and targets, let's consider a possible template for how to count and measure relative to abundant life. Again, this is meant to offer suggestions for guiding ministries, not absolutes for how we must measure our work as congregations.

SCORING ABUNDANT LIFE

Let's briefly review what we have learned about participating in abundant life so we can be certain that our template addresses everything we should count or measure:

1. Salvation is the greatest goodness people can enjoy. It entails rescuing people from the chaos and darkness that is too powerful for them and settling them in a place of abundance, wholeness, and harmony. Salvation is brought about by God in this world and the

next through the life, death, and resurrection of Jesus Christ. To experience this salvation in its fullest is to participate in abundant life, which involves both receiving the gift of God by faith and sharing the life God gives us with others.

2. Participating in abundant life includes improving people's standard of living by increasing their access to items they need to consume. Increasing this access can entail helping people directly or working to overcome structural issues that limit their income or ability to obtain needed goods and services.

3. Participating in abundant life includes improving people's quality of life by increasing their happiness. One of the best ways to do this is by providing people with a sense of belonging and acceptance through friendships and/or entrance into a community. A community that provides a purpose is even better.

4. Because improving people's standard of living and quality of living deal with the physical world only, there is no requirement for someone to be a follower of Jesus for them to engage in these activities. People can hold to any religion or no religion and still be life-giving to those in need.

5. For Christians, participating in abundant life also involves sharing the gospel, which is the good news that God has forgiven sin and overcome death through Jesus Christ. People are invited to receive forgiveness and eternal life by becoming disciples of Jesus. This eternal aspect of salvation is foundational for offering all other aspects of abundant life.

6. Disciples of Jesus are defined as those who participate in abundant life, both enjoying and sharing the various gifts of life with others. The greatest hope is that this sharing will result in others becoming disciples who will likewise enjoy all the aspects of abundant life and share them with others.

7. Disciples of Jesus can work with anyone of goodwill who desires to share any of the aspects of life with others. In doing this, participating in abundant life and working for the common good overlap each other.

Combining these insights with the lesson on making good goals with appropriate measurements, we can develop the following possible score cards for determining effectiveness in participating in abundant life.

Traditionally, statistical forms are for congregations to count their inputs and throughputs as an institutional organization. The score cards offered here differ by being defined with the impact in mind, which is the overarching goal. Within each goal there are several targets that count the specific activities, resources, immediate effects, and effects on people (throughputs, inputs, outputs, and outcomes) needed to reach the goal.

Another difference is that there are two sets of score cards. The first is for individual Christians. The second is for the entire congregation. The reason for this is that much of the work a congregation desires to accomplish is not done as a gathered body. Instead, it is accomplished by the individual Christians who participate in abundant life in their respective lives. To have a full sense of the difference that a local church is making, there must be a way of measuring the work of the church scattered as well as the church gathered. This work involves what the individual does both in their personal development and in their missional activities.

The idea is that individuals would have these score cards available for them to fill out each week. This process could be put online, provided through physical cards that are passed out and collected, or handled another way. The key issue is that the congregation would see what everyone was doing and have a way of measuring all that God was accomplishing through them.

I recognize that expecting people to track their daily lives and share that information is a big ask, especially when congregations have long shied away from making any significant demands on their members. Such a request would likely also be met with concerns over privacy. These sorts of issues would need to be adjudicated by the wisdom of each congregation. However, even if there was not a regular gathering of this data, just providing the score cards to people would be a way of helping change the culture of the local church. People would begin to recognize that participating in abundant life involves an intentional set of activities that touch on multiple aspects of their daily lives. That alone would be a positive step.

The importance of this discipleship formation for individual Christians became especially clear during the pandemic quarantines. When congregations were not capable of engaging in corporate acts of Christian witness, individual Christians and Christian families had to step up to be the visible Christian witness where they lived. Forming people to carry on this work moved from being a "next level" activity to an essential activity for every congregation.

You will notice larger spaces in several targets on the cards. This is intentional. While there are some broad goals and targets we can all share, contextual wisdom is called for to determine the best ways to measure salvific effectiveness in a specific location. What are the gifts, problems, and realities of the congregation and its setting? The congregation should be free to determine the exact ways it can best offer the abundant life of Christ where it is.

Another important caveat: the common assumption is that more is usually better. In this case, the more time, money, or effort put into a category, the more likely a person is participating in abundant life. This is not always the case. At times God may call us to step back from certain work. For example, new parents could well be more faithful stewards of the gift of life by spending less time volunteering for congregational ministries and more time at home with their infant. Someone who cannot leave the house for medical reasons may never join in corporate worship but could be a deeply committed prayer warrior. An entire congregation may be called to focus on a specific need in their neighborhood, leaving no bandwidth to support other worthy causes. These are not failures! The numbers matter insofar as they provide accountability for how God is calling a congregation or a specific Christian to serve.

To reiterate one more time: these are not absolutes. They are meant to prompt the congregation and individual Christians to think through how they are participating in abundant life in concrete and measurable ways. They can and should be revised to fit with how God is calling for that participation in this season.

INDIVIDUAL SCORE CARDS

The individual score cards focus on how individuals choose to accept, use, and share the abundant life that God makes available to them, especially as provided through the Christian community.

There are three goals for the individual: (1) to participate in abundant life with other Christians, (2) to grow in abundant life through personal formation as a Christian, and (3) to steward abundant life in daily life. These deal with the three broad ways that abundant life is made available to a person: as mediated through a Christian community, as accepted directly by the individual, and through stewarding the gifts of life well.

The goals, in this case, are equivalent to the outcomes discussed at the beginning of the appendix. The reason for this is that they each are broad measurements of the way the inputs, throughputs, and outputs affected the individual's life. The overall impact would be a vision of the individual becoming a mature Christian whose life is ordered around obedience to the great commandments: love God and love your neighbor as yourself.

Each goal is broad in scope and so requires several targets to measure it. None of these goals are able to be "completed," in these sense that a person could attain perfect participation in abundant life. However, the targets allow the person filling out the score cards to see how they are doing in relation to the goals. By filling out the score cards once, a person could get a snapshot of their participation in abundant life for that moment. By filling out the score cards regularly over weeks, months, or

Goal 1

Participate in abundant life with other Christians

INPUTS—Resources I put into the local church

of times I prayed for the church or people in it

# of hours and minutes I dedicated to participating
with people in the local church

# of dollars I gave to support the local church or people in it

Skills, talents, or gifts that I
used to support the local
church or people in it
—list these:

THROUGHPUTS—Activities to participate in abundant life offered to you by the local church

of times participated in corporate worship

# of times participated
in small group
—list type(s) of group(s):

# of times received Holy Communion

OUTPUTS—Activities I engaged in to help other Christians participate in abundant life

of times I was vulnerable about my faith
and life with another Christian informally

# of times I was vulnerable about my faith and life with
another Christian formally (as a mentor, mentee, or other
setting explicitly set aside to foster Christian discipleship)

# of times I confessed my sins to a fellow Christian this week

# of times I forgave someone this week

# of times I used my spiritual gifts to support
the Christian community—list which ones
(if helpful, use the list from 1 Corinthians 12):

# of times I used my resources to
support the Christian community
—list all (time, money, expertise, etc.):

Form A.2. Individual score card 1: Participating in abundant life with other Christians years, and then comparing these score cards over time, the person could see how that participation waxed and waned in specific ways.

The first score card deals with how individuals take initiative to engage with other Christians to participate in abundant life (see form A.2). Their inputs are the resources they invest in the congregation. They are provided activities by the congregation that allow them to improve their quality of life and that encourage them in discipleship. As they make use of these resources, their outputs are activities that show how they related in more intimate ways with other Christians.

These activities help deepen their participation in abundant life both in the world and eternally. It does the former by drawing them more deeply into relationships within their congregation. It does the latter by allowing them to claim the forgiveness offered through Jesus more fully. It also does the latter by allowing them to share the gifts of abundant life with others in the congregation through providing financial and relational support as well as by forgiving anyone who may have harmed them.

The second score card focuses on how the person is participating in abundant life in their personal devotion to God (see form A.3). One of the same resources (inputs) is kept from the first table: time. This is because the only resource needed to grow in personal devotion is uninterrupted time spent in the presence of God.

The throughputs measure the specific spiritual disciplines the person put their time into as part of their devotional activities. These disciplines allow for their improved quality of life through being in a more intimate relationship with God. It also allows for personal access to the assurance of forgiveness and eternal salvation God offers through Jesus Christ.

The outputs are descriptions of ways they have seen God work in their lives or situations in which they are still waiting on God to work. These outputs are measuring how God has worked through the person's devotional practices.

Goal 2

Grow in abundant life through personal formation as a Christian

INPUTS—Resources I put into my devotional life

of hours and minutes of uninterrupted time I dedicated
to personal devotion with God

THROUGHPUTS—Resources I received in the form of spiritual disciplines

of times I confessed my sins to God

# of hours and minutes I have spent in personal prayer

# of hours and minutes I have spent reading the Bible individually

# of meals skipped to fast

# of hours and minutes spent reading
/listening/studying about the Christian
faith—list topics studied:

# of hours and minutes spent in family devotions

# of hours and minutes spent in other
spiritual disciplines—list disciplines:

# of items I intentionally sought God's
will about—list items:

OUTPUTS—Situations where I observed or participated in God acting

of things I have prayed and/or fasted
about that I have seen God work in
—briefly describe what I have seen:

# of times I recognized the presence
of God—briefly describe what
I have seen:

# of things that are unresolved and
bothering my conscience—briefly
describe my struggle:

# of times I demonstrated the fruit of
the Spirit—briefly describe what
happened, drawing from
Galatians 5 to help:

Form A.3. Individual score card 2: Participating in abundant life through devotional practices

Goal 3

Steward abundant life in daily life

INPUTS—Resources I put into offering God's abundant life outside the church

of hours and minutes I spent praying for God's will
to be done outside the church

# of hours and minutes I dedicated to demonstrate God's
love to people outside the church

# of hours and minutes I dedicated to learn about where
abundant life is needed in the world—list what learned:

# of dollars I gave to demonstrate God's love to people outside the church

# of my possessions I used to demonstrate God's
love to people outside the church

Skills, talents, or gifts that I used to
demonstrate God's love to people
outside the church—list these:

THROUGHPUTS—Stewarded resources in a way that demonstrates abundant life

of people I was willing to be interrupted from my daily routine to help

# of people outside of the church I am praying
will come to the Christian faith

# of times I was vulnerable about my faith and life with another person

# of people from outside the church I have invited to a Christian event

# of places I volunteer in the
community to improve people's
standard of living—list these:

# of places I volunteer in the
community to improve people's
quality of life—list these:

# of times I used my resources to
meet someone's immediate
need—list needs met:

# of ways I engaged in civil society
(voted, wrote letter to elected official,
participated in demonstration, etc.)
—list these:

# of civic events I have attended (farmers' market, Fourth of July, local festival, etc.)—list these:	
# of times I prayed for issues occurring within the larger world	

OUTPUTS—Activities meant to invite people to experience aspects of abundant life

# of times I made an ethical decision informed by my faith—briefly describe the situation and where these were made (work, home, etc.):	
# of times I felt that God moved me to reach out to someone or intervene in a situation—briefly describe what happened:	
# of times I saw God's salvation take hold in a situation or in a person's life —briefly describe what happened:	
# of times I felt that a situation needed to be addressed by the church as a whole—briefly describe the need and what the church could do:	

Form A.4. Individual score card 3: Participating in abundant life through missional service. Page 2 of 2

The final score card measures how individuals are stewarding their resources in their daily lives as they relate to the world around them (see form A.4). The inputs are the resources that the person shared with others. This is connected to the person's growing awareness of the needs in the world.

The throughputs are activities the person undertook with a specific view to share the aspects of abundant life with others. The person could seek to improve other people's standard of living or quality of life by volunteering at a local shelter or by tutoring an at-risk student. The person could share the gospel of God's offer of forgiveness and eternal life through Jesus Christ through talking to a friend about their faith and inviting that friend to respond. The person might invite people from outside the local church to attend a Christian event, thereby offering those people the opportunity to hear the gospel and to connect with a community. These are all ways that the person engages in a process of being a faithful steward of the abundant life they have received while simultaneously participating more fully in that life.

Finally, the outputs look at the ways that the person sensed God's presence in the world. This helps them identify when they thought God was actively working through them or making them aware of situations in which they could more fully participate in abundant life by serving others.

Congregational Score Cards

The second set of score cards is for the congregation. In these cards, the inputs are the resources the congregation puts toward providing people opportunities to become more mature as disciples of Jesus Christ. The throughputs are the opportunities themselves, in the form of activities the congregation provides to help individuals more fully participate in abundant life. The outputs are the numbers of people that engage in these opportunities, along with the resources those individuals make available for the church to continue sharing abundant life with others. These score cards are not meant to measure the effectiveness of the congregation in generating support for itself but rather the effectiveness of the church in prompting others—whether they are inside the church or not—to share in Christ's abundant life by changing the way they live and use their resources.

As with the individual score cards, the overall impact the congregation desires is for people to become mature disciples of Jesus Christ who love God and love their neighbors as themselves. A person formed this way has personal assurance of salvation and becomes an agent of spreading abundant life to others.

Goal 1

Gather people to experience abundant life communally

INPUTS—Resources church provides to help people experience abundant life communally

# of hours and minutes of staff time dedicated to support people who gather communally inside the church

# of hours and minutes allotted for people to gather communally as a congregation

# of square feet of facility space dedicated for people to gather communally inside the church

# of church possessions dedicated to support people gathering communally inside the church

# of dollars budgeted to support people gathering communally inside the church

THROUGHPUTS—Activities provided to help people experience abundant life communally

# of opportunities to engage in corporate worship

# of small groups available —list type(s) of group(s) and number of each:

# of times Holy Communion was offered

# of prayer-focused ministries

# of opportunities to read the Bible and discuss it communally

# of introductory or confirmation classes

# of opportunities to learn about the Christian faith (Sunday school, Bible studies, etc.)—list these:

# of opportunities to learn about the spiritual disciplines

# of celebrations offered for the congregation (include parties, wedding receptions, or anything else your church considers a joyful celebration, possibly including liturgical acts)

# of opportunities in which fellowship was encouraged among the congregation either inside or outside of the church building

---

Form A.5. Congregational score card 1: Participating in abundant life communally. Page 1 of 2

OUTPUTS—Number of people affected by communal church activities

# of people who attended each corporate worship opportunity	
# of people who attend each of the small groups	
# who received Holy Communion	
# of people who pray communally	
# of people who read the Bible communally	
# of people who study communally	
# of adult/youth baptisms	
# of people in new member or confirmation classes	
# of new people welcomed into the community	
# confirmed	
# of infant/sponsored baptisms	
# of people who shared their testimony publicly at a church event (worship, small groups, etc.)	
# of dollars collected for use within the Christian community	

Form A.5. Congregational score card 1: Participating in abundant life communally. Page 2 of 2

The first score card includes metrics that are likely familiar to most church leaders (attendance in worship or in small groups, offerings collected, etc.). The reason for gathering these data is not the same as the reason we likely do it now. Usually these statistics are gathered to show the strength of the congregation as an institution. Sometimes they are then sent to be aggregated with other congregations' data to determine the strength of a judicatory or denomination. In such a case, the goal is to provide a baseline measurement for the institutional church. (See form A.5.)

In our case, the goal is not inward looking but rather outward looking toward how many people are participating in abundant life communally because of the ministry of the congregation. To determine this, we measure how many resources and opportunities the congregation provides people to live into the different aspects of abundant life with each other. The inputs show how many of the church's resources are dedicated to this. The throughputs are the activities these resources make possible, such as worship, study, and receiving the sacraments. The outputs are the number of people who have taken advantage of these opportunities as well as the amount of money people have shared so that the congregation can continue offering these opportunities to others. By shifting the goal to focus on salvation rather than institutional upkeep, the meaning behind these statistics becomes much different from how we are used to interpreting them.

One major difference between data collected with an impact rooted in abundant life rather than in institutional upkeep is that there is no reference to membership beyond the new member class. This is intentional. Membership can be helpful if it is used as a celebratory milestone for people who are more fully embracing abundant life in an intentional way. However, it is usually treated as a means of guaranteeing institutional support from individuals for the congregation and/or denomination. If this is its only use, then it is irrelevant to the goal of prompting individuals to participate more fully in abundant life.

The second score card is similar to the first one, taking the next step by asking how the congregation is helping people participate in abundant life more fully by forming them as disciples (see form A.6). The inputs are essentially the same as the ones in the first score card, looking at the congregation's resources that are dedicated to supporting people in their discipleship formation. The throughputs are opportunities the congregation offers people to practice more rigorous spiritual disciplines, such as discernment and fasting. There is a particular emphasis on the leadership of the congregation practicing these disciplines, as the leadership should set the example for participating in abundant life for the rest of the people. The outputs are ways leaders and other people in the congregation have seen God work.

One of these possible outputs is giving people an opportunity to question or doubt their beliefs within the congregation. This is important

Goal 2

Grow in abundant life through formation as disciples

INPUTS—Resources church provides to help people be formed as disciples

\# of hours and minutes of staff time dedicated to form people as disciples

\# of hours and minutes allotted for people to engage in intentional discipleship formation

\# of square feet of facility space dedicated for people to gather for discipleship activities

\# of possessions dedicated for people to gather for discipleship activities

\# of dollars budgeted to support discipleship formation

THROUGHPUTS—Activities church provides that form people as disciples

\# of opportunities to ask questions and express uncertainty or doubt without judgment

\# of times the church has been invited to fast together

\# of hours and minutes the congregational leadership spent in devotions together

\# of things the congregational leadership spent discerning God's will about—list these:

\# of ways congregational leaders are held accountable and encouraged to grow in their character as Christians

OUTPUTS—Ways people have demonstrated greater maturity as disciples

\# of things the congregation has prayed and/or fasted about that you have seen God work in—briefly describe what you have seen:

\# of times the congregation has recognized the presence of God—briefly describe what you have seen:

\# of people who have expressed doubt, questions, or struggles in the church

\# of leaders developed within the local church

\# of ways the congregation worked toward internal reconciliation when there was a disagreement

---

Form A.6. Congregational score card 2: Participating in abundant life through discipleship formation for two reasons. First, it allows for those who have not been Christian, but who have been attracted to the congregation because of opportunities to help offer salvation to others, a place to work out their beliefs over time. People are not expected to convert without thinking through what they believe salvation is and how Jesus relates to that. Second, a lack of opportunity to ask questions about faith can lead to "deconversion" as people reject the entire Christian faith because they are not given the space to question it. An intentional space for questioning and doubt will allow people to claim abundant life more fully, even if it takes longer for them to do it.

The final score card points to activities that are usually understood as outreach or missional activities by congregations (see form A.7). In the language we have been using, these activities are stewarding the aspects of abundant life in a way that invites others to accept that life. The inputs are the amount of resources and effort that people from a congregation collectively put into sharing abundant life. The throughputs measure the numbers and kinds of activities the congregation uses to improve people's standard of living and quality of life as well as evangelistic efforts in which they shared the gospel. The outputs show the results of these efforts, counting those who have had their lives improved and those who have proclaimed faith in Jesus Christ.

While not overtly stated, an important feature of the congregational score cards is that they contain a discipleship system in them. A discipleship system is a process that moves people into greater Christian maturity, including an invitation for those outside the church to consider the Christian faith, ways for those who are interested in the faith to experience the life of a Christian without having to commit to Christ initially, entry points for those who do desire to commit to Christ, and ways to grow more deeply in the Christian faith as a disciple who stewards the gifts of abundant life. The parts of this system are spread throughout the congregational cards, but they are all included. They are all needed because each invites people to a fuller experience of salvation.

Goal 3

Be an agent of abundant life for the community and larger world

INPUTS—Resources provided to share abundant life outside the church

# of hours and minutes of staff time dedicated to being outside the church

# of hours and minutes allotted for church people to work together outside the church

# of ministries that intentionally focus their work outside the church for the sake of the community

# of possessions dedicated to work outside the church for the sake of the community

# of dollars budgeted to support work outside the church for the sake of the community

# of hours and minutes spent in collective prayer for those outside the church

THROUGHPUTS—Activities that equip people to be in witness outside the church

# of times pastor has spoken about evangelism

# of ways the church has invited people from the community to attend it

# of times the pastor of the church has set aside time to be available and listen in the community around the church

# of ways the church has listened to the needs of people outside the church

# of programs set up by the church to meet the immediate needs of people in the neighborhood

# of dollars spent in accordance with the church's mission outside the church

% of total expenditures used for offering abundant life outside the church

# of work hours spent in accordance with the church's mission outside the church

% of total work hours used for offering salvation outside the church

# of ways in which the pastor or church provided guidance on how to use personal resources according to Christian ethics

# of social issues raised by the church

Form A.7. Congregational score card 3: Participating in abundant life through missions. Page 1 of 2

# of opportunities church provided to learn about current events	
# of opportunities church provided for engaging in work meant to bring social reform—list these:	

OUTPUTS—Ways the local church worked to provide abundant life outside the church

# of new visitors to a church event	
# of new visitors to a church event who were followed up with	
# of new church visitors who returned	
# of people who made a new decision to become disciples of Jesus Christ	
# of missionaries supported by the church	
# of collaborations the church has with other organizations working for social change	
# of ways the church has been visible to the surrounding community (hosting a booth at a fair, being in a march, being in the news, etc.) —list these:	
# of people whose standard of living the church helped improve	
# of people whose quality of life the church helped improve	

Form A.7. Congregational score card 3: Participating in abundant life through missions. Page 2 of 2

MEASURING SALVATION

Undoubtedly there are people who will argue that there are line items missing from these measurements, that the measurements are too stilted toward particular forms of abundant life, or that the inputs, throughputs, outputs, and outcomes are not right. These are all valid points. I offer these score cards not as a finalized, absolute tool for what to count and measure but as a (hopefully) helpful step in the direction of reframing the way we often think about congregational statistics. Instead of always having them point back to the institutional structure, I am offering a model that points toward measuring the way the congregation encourages people to participate in abundant life. I am shifting the congregation from being the end point of the metrics to being the means through which people are formed to be participants in abundant life.

I expect these score cards to be revised to make them useful for congregations and individuals. For example, in a conversation I had with a church leader whose congregation was developing its own score cards for individual members, I learned that they had found it was necessary to allow for the metrics to be modified based on personality types. They realized they had tended to include metrics that strongly favored extroverts, leaving introverts feeling as though they had little to offer. Introverts who quietly serve to improve others' standard of living are just as important as extroverts who are publicly proclaiming the gospel. This congregation wanted to capture that point in its metrics. Congregations should be free to modify these cards to fit with their context, size, theology, gifts, resources, and the personalities of the people in them.

Theology can also be a contentious point. With more than a decade of experience teaching evangelism, I know that intra-Christian disagreement can be filled with vitriol. I also know that any attempt to do what I am doing, which is to argue for bridging different views of salvation, will likely be met with skepticism and pushback. Those whose theology trends toward bringing mercy and justice to people on earth will claim I am giving Christians a way to bail out of these responsibilities by making it possible for local churches to say they are participating in abundant life through just proclaiming the gospel so people can experience eternal life. What good is eternity if it comes at the expense of a miserable existence on earth, especially if that misery is caused by unjust political, social, and economic systems that could be overcome if the church committed itself to intervene and change these things? Those whose theology emphasizes eternal life will likely state that I am endangering people's souls by calling for churches to see standard of living and quality of life as equally part of salvation. What good is it if someone is well fed and living in a just society in this world if they never repent and claim the forgiveness offered through Jesus Christ? Their brief temporal life will give way to an eternity apart from God's goodness.

An individual congregation may be more gifted to lead people to eternal life or toward an improved standard of living or a higher quality of life. Good enough. That does not mean that they must reject or ignore the other forms of ministry that lead to other aspects of abundant life. In such a case, the congregation might choose to link with other congregations in the area or even with secular agencies that will make the fullness of abundant life available. No one congregation has to offer everything, but every congregation should recognize the multifaceted nature of God's abundant life and have some means of pointing people toward participating in all of it. That is more my point: all Christians and Christian congregations should recognize, articulate, and find some way to be accountable to participating in all the aspects of abundant life.

Preparing a congregation to form people to participate in abundant life takes significant internal work. The leadership must set the example by being engaged in spiritual disciplines, and they must offer the people opportunities to be formed as disciples. Only out of this committed formation will the fullness of salvation be felt and enjoyed by the congregation so that, in turn, it can overflow to others.

In the end, can we measure our participation in abundant life? Partially. Abundant life is ultimately God's work, which we can neither control nor reduce to human activity. It also involves transforming people, altering their character to make it holy. In that sense, we cannot measure it beyond observing the outcomes in people's lives over time.

However, we can measure the ways we participate in abundant life. We can measure if we are sharing resources with those who are in need, making that a priority in our budgets and calendars. We can measure whether we are taking time to befriend the lonely and are welcoming new people into our communities. We can even measure whether we are taking the time to linger in the presence of God through spiritual disciplines and whether we are sharing the gospel with others. What we can measure is our stewardship of the abundant life God has given us.

General Index

abundant life, 10-12, 185-87
  communal, 120, 145
  and discipleship formation, 170
  and the Divine Liturgy, 164-68
  experience of salvation, 30, 33
  explicated by standard of living, quality of life,
    and eternal life, 16, 49, 57, 146
  and metrics, 50-52, 181-85
  missional, x, 20, 37, 39-40, 49, 78, 94-95,
    104-5, 142
  participated in by those who are not
    Christian, 14, 30, 91-92, 149, 155, 158
  and sacrifice, 75-77
  See also common good; kingdom of God;
    salvation; stewardship; suffering
Aldred, Ray, 46
Aquinas, Thomas, Saint, 124-26, 128-29
Better Life Index, 18, 182-83
Bowler, Kate, 37-38
Brueggemann, Walter, 61, 65-68
Catholic Relief Services (CRS), 87-90, 94
chaos, 77, 101, 128, 133, 136, 161, 170-72
  in Hebrew Scriptures, 65, 67-69
  in the New Testament, 70-72, 92, 185
  overcome by salvation, 92, 138, 145, 160, 185
Chaoskampf, 61-63, 72
Choge-Kerama, Emily J., 43
Collier, Paul, 99-101, 181
common good, 13-14
  and eternity, 137-38, 158
  and participating in abundant life, x, 12-15,
    25-26, 49-50, 132-34, 187
  valued by those who are not Christian, 78, 86,
    112-14, 121-22, 126
  working toward as Christian witness, 41-42,
    46-47, 53-55, 101, 126, 163-64, 180
community, 52, 63, 112, 126-28, 164
  the church as, 43, 73, 75, 96, 119-20, 131-32,
    149, 151, 168, 189
  as the context for mission, 44, 97
  and Jesus, 114-18
  as a means of providing relationship, 12, 45,
    71, 74, 77, 133, 137, 182, 186
community organizing, 118, 128, 163
Cone, James, 5
consumerism, 98, 101-4, 132, 147
Covid-19, 4-5, 63, 108-9, 161, 170
Croasmun, Matthew, 12-13, 53-54
Crouch, Andy, 170
Demir, Melikşah, 129
discipleship, 40, 137, 188
  becoming disciples, 70, 156, 157, 169, 186
  making disciples, 2, 72-74, 146, 160
  and partnering with secular organizations,
    158, 187
  and sharing abundant life, 145
divine judgment, 3, 7, 26, 33, 137-40, 159-60,
  161-63, 166-67
  and faith in Jesus Christ, 140-42
  and good deeds, 142-44
Divine Liturgy, 27, 164-68
Easterlin Paradox, 111
Eastern Orthodox, 31-33, 94, 164-68
eternal life, 18-23,
  and divine judgment, 136-38, 142-47
  in the Divine Liturgy, 27, 164, 167-68
  and faith in Jesus, 140-42
  linked to standard of living and quality of life,
    54, 94, 116, 134, 142-47, 159, 202-3
  metrics, 174, 182, 186
  ministry of Jesus, 11, 77, 128
  missional call to share, 12, 25, 30, 70, 73-74,
    78
evangelism, 2, 6-8, 43, 132, 160, 163, 164, 169
  See also discipleship; gospel: sharing
Evangelism Equation, 182
Floyd, George, 4
Fluker, Walter, 126-27, 131

friendship, 111, 113-15, 125, 128-31, 134, 145-46, 182, 186
    and befriending others, 113-14, 131, 137, 160, 204
    and betrayal, 62, 67
Gabaitse, Rosina Mmannana, 44
Global Happiness Policy Report, 17
Good Shepherd, 10-11
gospel, x, 9-10, 12, 15, 35, 51-52, 78, 116, 120, 136, 149, 153, 164, 195
    reduced, 58, 146, 155-56
    sharing, 2, 14, 26, 30, 41, 43, 55, 70, 96, 105, 160, 163, 186, 194, 200, 203, 204
Great Commission, 72-74
Greatest Commandments, 144
happiness, 17-18, 22-23, 76, 107, 133-34, 139, 159-60, 182, 186
    and Aristotle, 121-22
    eudaimonic, 110-11
    hedonic, 109, 128-30
    hedonic adaptation, 110-11, 130
    and John Locke, 122-23
    and Plato, 121
    and Thomas Aquinas, 124-26
Hebrew Scriptures, 26, 60-65, 69-70, 72
Hirsch, Alan, 9, 39-40, 58, 136-37, 160
humanitarianism, 164
    humanitarian agencies, 19, 50, 79, 87, 104, 180-81
    humanitarian aid, 2, 86, 88, 90-92, 94-98, 100, 104, 138, 148, 160, 163
John the Baptist, 16
Jones, E. Stanley, 26, 155-58
Journal of Happiness Studies, 129-30
kingdom of God, 69-78, 92-95, 138, 142, 147, 152, 157, 163
liberation, 5, 45-46
loneliness, 4, 107-9, 114, 116, 126, 133, 138, 161
MacIntyre, Alasdair, 126-27, 131
Majority World, 42-43, 47, 55, 57-58, 169
Martínez-Olivieri, Jules A., 44-45
McCance-Katz, Elinore, 108
McMahon, Darin, 22, 86
Médecins Sans Frontières (MSF), 87-90
Mercy Me, 29
metanarrative, 8, 37, 49, 103
metrics, 27, 42, 50-52, 162, 169, 173-74, 180-81, 185, 203
mission, 12
    avoid being co-opted, 138
    and humanitarian aid, 86-91, 104, 148,
    God's mission, 14, 57, 76, 120

    and Jesus, 20, 70, 72-74, 77, 136, 142, 155
    metrics, 173-75
    part of abundant life, x, 12, 30, 36-39, 40, 49, 95, 100, 105, 115, 132, 146
    work of the church, 15, 19
Moon, W. Jay, 169
Negative Endogenous Growth Theory, 111
Nelson, Mark, 9, 39-40, 58, 136-37, 160
New Testament, 26, 60, 69-72, 74-76, 138-39
Newbigin, Lesslie, 26, 149-58
Organization for Economic Cooperation and Development (OECD), 17-18, 182
Palamas, St. Gregory, 41-42
Paul, Evens, 1-3
Peace of Westphalia, 24-25
people of goodwill, 3, 10, 13, 15, 25-26, 64, 78, 89, 120, 137-38, 158, 163, 169, 172, 187
pluralism, 53-56, 113
poverty, 82-87, 90, 92, 95, 97, 99-101, 111-14, 150, 184-85
prosperity gospel, 34, 37-41
Psalms, 65-68, 75
public engagement, 24-26, 42, 68, 169
    and discourse, 53-55
quality of life, 17-18
    community of the church, 119-20
    consequences of low quality of life, 107-10
    in the Divine Liturgy, 27, 164, 167-68
    God's desire to improve, 37-38, 41, 60
    metrics, 50-52, 180-82
    and the ministry of Jesus, 70-77, 116-18
    missional call to improve, 68-70, 78
    as a positive feedback loop, 113-14, 134
    and *shalom*, 64
    and standard of living, 81, 106-7, 111
    See also community organizing; happiness; loneliness
racism, 4-5, 63, 127, 161
Reformed theology, 31-33
Rendle, Gil, 173-77, 181
repentance, 46, 119
resurrection of Jesus Christ, x, 19-20, 28-29, 35-36, 39, 56-58, 70-73, 119-20, 124, 141-42, 185
Ricoeur, Paul, 66
SAI-Haiti, 1-2
salvation, 9-10
    cosmic, 41
    earthly, 2, 61, 63-65, 92, 162, 203
    experienced, 3, 12, 14, 21, 23, 26, 29-30, 32-37, 39, 44-49, 50, 55, 57-59, 63, 81, 101, 105, 114, 120, 169, 186, 202

history, 63, 69
holistic, x, 3, 5, 10, 12, 26, 33, 43, 78, 109, 136
reduced, 9-10, 35, 41, 42, 45, 58, 137-38,
159-60, 204
See also eternal life
secularism, 3, 24-26, 41-42, 48-49, 53-55, 87, 98,
100, 162-64, 171
aid agencies, 91, 95, 146-49, 160, 168, 180,
183, 204
as a descriptor of culture, 9-10, 12-15, 18, 21,
23, 27, 39, 50-52, 56-57, 137, 169
and missionaries, 150-58
Seversen, Beth, 131-32
sin, 11, 13, 31-32, 62-63, 69, 128, 155
and death, 14, 35, 170
and forgiveness by God through Jesus, 11, 26,
73, 140-42, 145, 159, 164, 166, 168, 186, 191,
194, 203
and judgment, 3, 137
saved from, 36, 45, 70-73, 136, 140-42, 163
standard of living, 15, 16-17, 25, 30, 80-82
and consumerism, 101-4
in the Divine Liturgy, 27, 164, 167-68
God's desire to improve, 38, 41, 60
metrics, 50-52, 180-84
and the ministry of Jesus, 70-77, 92-93, 96
missional call to improve, 68-70, 73, 94-95
poverty, 83-85

public discourse, 53
and quality of life, 111
and *shalom*, 64
and stewardship, 97-98
See also humanitarianism
stewardship, 104-5
of creation, 36
and God's judgment, 138-39, 144
of the gospel message, 26
metrics, 189, 194-95, 200, 204
of physical resources, 81, 97-98, 100, 145-46,
159, 163
Stone, Bryan, 148-49, 155
suffering, 39-40
alleviation of, 51-52, 71, 81
human condition requiring salvation, 61, 65-69
willingness of disciples of Jesus to suffer,
39-41, 74-77
Taylor, Charles, 9
United Nations Human Development Index, 17,
82, 107, 180
United Nations Sustainable Development Goals,
84-86, 183-84
Volf, Miroslav, 12-13, 53-55
Wesley, John, 103, 120
Wesleyan/Arminian theology, 32-34
woman at the well, 117-18, 128, 133
World Happiness Report, 17, 107

Scripture Index

OLD TESTAMENT

Genesis
2:17, 35

Leviticus
13:45-46, 96
15:19-27, 96

Psalms
3:1, 67
6:6-7, 67
23, 167
30:5, 161
34:18, 110
38:11, 67
41:9, 67
82:3-4, 79
109:16, 110
147:3, 110

Isaiah
11:6-9, 64
61:1, 110
64:5, 59

Malachi
3:9-12, 134

NEW TESTAMENT

Matthew
5:11-12, 76
5:45, 13
6:31-32, 16
6:31-33, 70
7:21, 142
8:1-4, 96
8:12, 139
9:18-22, 96
10:8, 40, 74
10:28, 139
12:30, 138
13:24-30, 139
13:42, 139
13:47-49, 139

13:50, 139
22:13, 139
22:38-39, 144
24:45, 97
24:47, 97
24:51, 98, 139
25, 144
25:1-13, 144
25:14-30, 144
25:21, 160
25:31-32, 139
25:31-46, 94, 138, 144
28:18-20, 73

Mark
1:40-45, 96
3:33-35, 117
5:25-34, 96
8:36, 106
9:38-41, 52
9:40, 137
10:17, 59
10:29-30, 77, 116
10:45, 51
10:52, 117
12:34, 147
16:15-18, 73

Luke
3:11, 16
4, 44
4:18-19, 44
5:12-16, 96
6:32-35, 51
6:43-45, 52
8:43-48, 96
10:25, 59
11:20, 71
15:3-7, 11
16:19-31, 139
16:26, 139
17:11-19, 96
17:20-21, 71
18:18, 59
24:46-49, 73

John
3:16, 135, 136, 138, 159
4:1-42, 117
4:6, 117
4:7, 117
4:29, 118
4:39-42, 118
10:10, 10, 53
10:11-15, 11
10:27, 11
10:28, 11
11:23-26, 19
13:3-5, 74
17:15-19, 154
20:21-23, 73

Acts
1:7-8, 73
2:4, 119
2:37, 59
2:38, 119, 140
2:41, 119
2:42-47, 119
4:12, 141
5:41, 76
6:1, 74
11:1-18, 75
13:38-39, 141

Romans
5:18-21, 141
6:8, 141
8, 20
8:18, 40
8:31-39, 21
10:9-10, 142

1 Corinthians
3:11-15, 143
3:21-23, 40
3:22, 157
12, 190
15, 28
15:35, 28

15:52-57, 141
15:53, 28
16:1-4, 74

2 Corinthians
4:17, 40
5:10, 143
8, 74
8:2-4, 75

Galatians
5, 192

Ephesians
2:8-9, 27
3:20, 58

Philippians
1:21-25, 20
4:2-3, 75

Hebrews
9:27, 140
9:28, 140

James
2:1-4, 74
2:14-17, 94

1 Peter
4:12-13, 39
2 Peter
3:7, 140

1 John
3:2, 29
4:17, 140

Revelation
4:6, 72
15:2, 72
20:11-15, 143

Also by Mark R. Teasdale

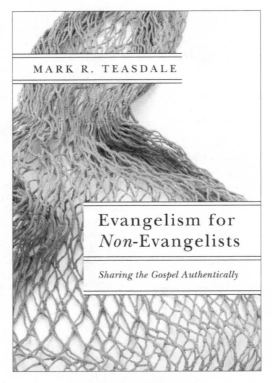

Evangelism for Non-Evangelists
978-0-8308-5166-9